HOOSIERS

HOOSIERS

THE
FABULOUS
BASKETBALL LIFE
OF INDIANA

Phillip M. Hoose

VINTAGE BOOKS

A DIVISION OF RANDOM HOUSE

NEW YORK

A VINTAGE ORIGINAL

Published in the United States by Random House, Inc., New York,
and simultaneously
in Canada by Random House of Canada Limited, Toronto.

Library of Congress Cataloging-in-Publication Data
Hoose, Phillip M., 1947–
  Hoosiers: the fabulous basketball life of Indiana
  "A Vintage original"—T.p. verso.
  1. Basketball—Indiana—History. I. Title.
GV885.72.I6H66   1986   796.32'3'09772   86-40170
ISBN 0-394-74778-X

Text design by Robert Bull

Manufactured in the United States of America

10 9 8 7 6 5 4 3 2

To Shoshana

ACKNOWLEDGMENTS

I would first like to thank the more than two hundred players, coaches, fans and administrators who took the time to talk with me. For extra help, especially in Indiana, I thank Dale Glenn, Darwin, Tim and Peggy Hoose, Al Harden, Mark Maxwell, Norm Held, Grace Hine, Jerry Birge, Kevin Smith, Marcus Stewart, Tom Roach, Sam Alford, Ray Crowe, Patricia Roy, Rick Mount, Gary Holland, Bob Denari, Harley Sheets and Bob Plump. Robert Boyle, Stuart Schmitz, Ann Harris and especially my agent, Philip Spitzer, gave me much-needed early encouragement. My good friend Alan Reinhardt offered wonderful comments on drafts and steered me tactfully away from the first person.

All Hoosiers should thank Dr. Herb Schwomeyer for his decades of research and documentation of basketball in Indiana. Almost singlehandedly, he has preserved an important part of Indiana's cultural history. I am deeply grateful to my mother, Patti Williams, for transcribing dozens of tapes magnificently and in short order. It's a wonder she can still hear.

Above all, I thank my wife, Shoshana, for giving me this book. She did the work of two parents while my mind was in Anderson or Milan and still had the skill and patience to help me with the manuscript.

CONTENTS

HOOSIERS

INTRODUCTION

One night not long ago, in a bar in Laconia, New Hampshire, I struck up a conversation with the couple at my table while the band was taking a break. The guy, a tax lawyer, said he was from Lafayette, Indiana. I looked at him carefully. He had to be close to my age. Finally I asked him: "Where'd you go to school?" Though he held two college degrees, he answered with the name of his high school, a good sign. "Central Catholic," he replied, "how about you?" "Speedway," I told him. There was a pause. "Henry Ebershoff?" I ventured. "Tom Smith," he countered, each of us naming a mid-sixties star of the other's team.

This has happened scores of times since I left Indiana in 1971. I am part of a great diaspora of Hoosiers out there, alumni and alumnae of "Hoosier Hysteria," one of thousands who have left the homeland but still carry around in their heads a strange goulash of names of people and towns: Cigarree Dunn and Theosee Nunn. Junior Gee from Loogootee and Dick ("T-Bone") Graf. Gnaw Bone and Stoney Lonesome. Oscar. Attucks. Milan. Jimmy Rayl. Bobby Plump.

3

The word "Lebanon" crops up in the news a thousand times and, for us, so does the fleeting image of Rick Mount. Likewise, Peru is Kyle Macy. Eugene Debs may have come home to Terre Haute to die, but the town *means* Harley, Arley and Uncle Harold.

Indiana is basketball's hometown. It is nearly a century of Friday nights, with everything but maybe the theater closed down, signs in the windows turned around, everything deathly still but the oversized gym, pulsating with heat and light.

Each March it is the state tourney—a month-long state fair, a celebration of athletic democracy attended by over a million people. In Indiana, unlike almost everywhere else, every high school in the state, no matter how big or little, plays in the same tourney. Given a chance to throw a haymaker, little schools regularly send teams from schools ten times their sizes sprawling in the sawdust. I, like most Hoosiers, will go to my grave able to recite the tourney's four rounds: sectionals, regionals, semistate, state.

In many places, basketball's operative community has become the playground, patches of glass-strewn asphalt where kids struggle for a few square feet of dignity. Of course, basketball means just as much to a kid trying to scrape up a reputation in Harlem as it does to a junior forward at Evansville Bosse, maybe more. But the playground means little to the everyday life of a community, to the thousands of workers and tenants and parishioners who live around the courts.

In Hoosierland, the pulse of winter life is the high school team, the Sabbath is Friday night, and the temple is your home gym. It's a place where you grew up, a room where, if you really had to, you could find your parents, and where you can look after your children. It's a place that others call

4

"the snake pit," or "the lion's den," but for you it's a place to gather with most of the people you know for a common, assumed, unspoken purpose: to root.

The patterns, the rhythms of the game become a part of your makeup. You can be talking to your neighbor or glancing at the scoreboard or trying to spot your daughter, and still, in that setting, a double dribble or an extra step registers like a skipped heartbeat.

You first saw the five players who are out there with your school's name on their jerseys long ago, as gangly children. All these years, you and your neighbors have been sizing them up like golden retriever pups, observing that their feet are big or remembering that their father was once fast. For years, over beers at night and coffee in the morning, you have been trying to predict their adult height, convincing each other that there is one growth spurt left in your junior center.

You pray that they will ripen together in the tourney, that God will bear these kids through the sectionals, and the regionals, and the semistate—maybe all the way to Indianapolis. Stranger things have happened, you tell each other. Look what happened to Milan. One thing is sure: God alone can keep the referees from ruining the harvest.

At the end of the bench is your coach, the leader of your tribe. The day he came, two years ago, after the school board sent the last coach packing, a whole lot of people went over to help him move in, mainly for the chance to look him over. His wife seemed a little standoffish then, but she's warmed up a little. He's done pretty well so far, although he still has a tendency to waste time-outs.

When you live in Indiana, everyone brags that it is the best basketball state, and yet it is hard to know until you leave and everything seems wrong. Outside Indiana, the

Welcome to Holland. *(Tom Roach)*

Welcome to Warsaw. *(Herb Schwomeyer, Hoosier Hysteria and Hersteria, Inc.)*

Welcome to Southport. *(Herb Schwomeyer, Hoosier Hysteria and Hersteria, Inc.)*

Welcome to Loogootee. *(Phillip M. Hoose)*

high school basketball section of the local sports page looks like the obituaries. Nobody even knows when the local teams play. Restaurant walls are bare of team-photo calendars.

But the biggest shock of all is to walk into a high school gym in North Carolina or California or Manhattan. There might be a few rows of bleachers on one or two sides, but my God, you wonder, where does everyone sit?

This is the story of the basketball life of Indiana. Ever since 1893, when a Presbyterian minister taught the people of Crawfordsville to throw a ball into a feed sack which hung from a forged iron hoop, Indiana has lived and breathed basketball in the winter. This is the story of a century of games and teams that have influenced every aspect of life in Indiana communities.

This is the story of Anderson, Indiana, whose multitudes of laid-off auto workers found comfort in the high school bleachers one desolate winter. It is Onward, whose 118 citizens defended their school—and their team—against sixty-seven state troopers and kept it alive for two years on chicken dinners. It is the ninety-two students of Greenfield who walked out for three days in support of their fired basketball coach. It is a house in flames in Washington and a barn burning in Holland.

This is the story of the state in which you can find eighteen of America's twenty biggest high school gyms. It is the story of towns desperate to build a gym big enough to snatch away the home court advantage in the tourney from the next town over, of community corporations and bond drives for the new gym, of WPA workers installing bleachers instead of building bridges during the Great Depression.

It is a movement by Gary fans in the early '50s to secede from Indiana to Illinois, where the referees were known to have better vision. It is a Muncie preacher assuring his troubled flock in 1929 that favoring a weaker team against Muncie Central "would be unsportsmanlike of God." It is a coach who signed a one-year contract requiring ten victories but stuck on nine going into the tourney.

It is the story of an all-black high school, established at a time when the Ku Klux Klan seized political control of Indiana, developing teams so dominant that whites called for neighborhood schools to head off a basketball dynasty in Indianapolis.

"Hoosier Hysteria," as Indiana's affliction is known locally, is a man named Bobby Plump whose sleep is still interrupted by barroom callers who want to talk about a shot he made over thirty years ago.

Hoosierland is Judi Warren and her Warsaw teammates who refused to come in and cook, or to accept inferior facilities, and who made Indiana respect them on their own terms. It is Larry Bird, who would not let his older brothers shoo him home or the pundits in Indianapolis diminish him. It is fathers encouraging their sons to repeat grades so they can develop their game. It is the state's obsessive fascination with Indiana University coach Bobby Knight. It is Oscar Robertson, whose undeniable greatness made whites regard blacks in a new way.

Before plunging, the reader has a right to know what the word "Hoosier" means. Unfortunately, the meaning is lost to the ages. James Whitcomb Riley, canonized as "the Hoosier poet," was often asked to define the word and gave what may be the most recent definition. "The early settlers were vicious fighters," Riley explained to one scribbling interviewer, "and they not only gouged and scratched, but frequently bit off noses and ears. This was so ordinary an affair that a settler coming into a barroom on a morning after a fight, and seeing an ear on the floor, would merely push it aside with his foot and carelessly ask, 'Who's y' ear?' "

For our purposes, a Hoosier is one who is drawn toward Friday nights and the month of March like the tides to a full moon. As James Naismith, the inventor of basketball, put it not long before he died in 1939, "Basketball really had its origin in Indiana, which remains today the center of the sport." A half-century later, it still is. This is the story of basketball's grass roots.

1

BASKETBALL TOWN

"If I had to take a disbeliever to just one place I'd take 'em to Anderson High School."

—HERB SCHWOMEYER,
the "Hoosier Hysteria Historian"

———————————

Ron Porter's ear is mashed against a telephone receiver. "Turn it up, Earl!" he screams at the bartender 1,200 miles away. Between the bedlam at the Olympia Lounge back in Anderson and the noise at the Astrodome, where the Boston Celtics are playing the Houston Rockets, Porter can barely hear.

It is February 1982. Driven from Anderson by the collapsing auto industry, Porter and his roommate, Ron James, arrived in Houston six months ago looking for cars to sell. The summer and fall were all right, but now it is winter— although it doesn't feel like it—and back home the Indians are playing Highland in the Wigwam right now, *right now* for the sectional title. As Larry Bird and Moses Malone go at it, Porter is thinking, my God, this is the first Indiana high school basketball tourney I've missed since 1954, when I was ten years old: the monkey's coming down hard.

By halftime, he can't take it any longer. Overcome, he

sprints up to a booth, jams some coins in a slot and dials Earl Alger at the Olympia. Alger knows exactly what to do, for he's known Ron Porter a long time, and he's had cases like this before. He places the receiver tight against a radio, turns up the broadcast, and goes back to mixing drinks. Porter never returns to his seat.

Ron Porter is one of a diaspora of fifty or so Anderson High School alumnae—"Old Indians," they are called—who depend on these long distance radio hookups each March during the tourney. There are cheaper habits. When the Indians make it all the way to the final game, as they have three of the last seven years, it means eight two-hour calls. Porter's Astrodome call alone cost him "only about twenty-five dollars, weekend rates."

Anderson, Indiana, is the hottest basketball town on earth, the epicenter of grass-roots basketball, where The Game has been celebrated—lived is a better word—on Fridays after sundown for nearly a century. Seventeen families have held season tickets to Anderson High School games since the Great Depression. The townspeople have gussied up in red and green—Indian colors—to share popcorn and cheers and dances and songs that haven't changed for longer than anyone can remember. Many Andersonians can best mark the events of their lives by remembering what grade a star player was in at the time, or how the Indians did in the state tourney, year after year.

Unlike a college hoop town like Chapel Hill or Westwood or Lexington, where student fans wash in and out like a bore tide, Anderson's 65,000 residents stay put all year and live, breathe, talk, bet, eat but never digest basketball. Travel around Indiana and ask coaches and players to name the hotbed of hotbeds, and you'll hear a lot of replies like, "We have great fans, but those people in Anderson are crazy."

Anderson is a GM town whose residents spend their secular hours cranking out headlights and windows and doors. Anderson's economy depends almost entirely on how quickly we buy Chevies and Pontiacs and Buicks. At one time the city, with a large and stable labor force and low taxes, was promoted as "the next Detroit." But in the late '70s and early '80s, when high interest rates and foreign competition hurt the auto industry throughout America, Anderson nearly collapsed.

Within a brief period, GM laid off 5,000 workers, Nicholson File and Anaconda Wire moved out, and small job shops dried up. Soon Anderson had the highest unemployment rate in the nation, over 22 percent. While welders and assembly workers stayed home, salespeople like Ron Porter headed off for places like Houston, looking for showrooms with some action. Daybreak found the citizens of Anderson clinging to The Game.

In that desolate winter the bleachers became pews. Anderson High School sold 5,600 season tickets, nearly twice as many as the NBA's Indiana Pacers, and crosstown rivals Highland and Madison Heights each sold several thousand more. When all three schools had home games on the same night, one of every four Anderson residents was in a gym, sheltered in tradition. In the Wigwam, four generations huddled together in warmth and light and ritual. The old problems—how to break Kokomo's press or contain Muncie Central's guards—left no room for brooding about the future.

Even jobless families could afford eighteen dollars for a season ticket, a pass to twelve winter evenings of blessed relief. "I mean, things were bad around here," says Anderson Mayor Jack McMahan. "I'm talking about real human needs. But basketball was the great stabilizing factor. I'm very serious about this. Even if they didn't have a job, people could look forward to the games. When snowstorms closed down the city government and the library, I've seen people walk down the railroad track in two feet of snow to get to the gym."

Anderson High had already outgrown two gyms by 1925, when the doors were opened to the original Wigwam. Anderson's children hoarded pennies to buy bonds to pay for the Wigwam, the gym that would at last be big enough for everyone. The bonds were hawked with the patriotic fervor of the great World War I bond drives. Seating over 5,000, the Wigwam was to be the Gym to end all Gyms.

It was too small from the first whistle. The town lived with it until the winter of 1958, when it burned to the ground. There are many who believe it was finally torched by a frustrated fan, an individual who would almost certainly be pardoned—if not decorated—today, given the roominess of the new Wigwam, which soon began to rise out in the old parking lot.

Today, from across Lincoln Street, Anderson High, built in 1910, looks from the front like a tough old tortoise straining beneath an oversized carapace. The burden is best examined from the parking lot behind the school. The new Wigwam is an enormous mint-green cube with an Indian's head emblazoned on the side. Judging from the size of the building alone, it's plain to see that this time they got it right.

Naturally, it is more a temple than a gym. Seating 9,000,

it cost over two million dollars even in 1960. Coach Norm Held and athletic director Robert Belangi are proud to guide a guest through the Wigwam's weight rooms and video room, past an Olympic-sized pool and into the locker room for a glimpse of pantries full of new shoes and practice uniforms and bright orange balls. "I have a sister who coaches at a major college," says Belangi, tucking a uniform back into place. "She says she's never seen anything like this."

Voices seem to lower automatically in the gym itself, as voices will when you enter a sanctuary. This is a good room for Norm Held. Forceful, blue-eyed and curly-haired, he looks and even sounds like an evangelist, something in the broadened O's and repetition of his speech. His words fill up the space. "What I call coaching is moti*va*tion," he says, "keeping kids ex*cite*d about playing, ex*cite*d about staying eligible, ex*cite*d about going on to college and doing something special with their lives." Gazing around this mighty tribute to a town's special obsession, Held states the obvious: "Any other high school coaching job in the nation would be a step down."

Held knows something about the coaching ladder's lower rungs. A map of his early career reads like a Greyhound tour of very rural Illinois. Stops included East Lynn (41 students), Patomic (90 students), Catlin (180 students) and bigger schools in Park Forest and Danville. Though Held twice took Danville to the Illinois state finals, a falling-out with a new administration left Held frustrated and itchy again.

"I was playing tennis one afternoon with a coaching friend and he said, 'What do you think about Anderson?' I didn't know much about it, but I came over here and applied. I had heard of Anderson High, but I sure didn't know about all of *this*. I remember in the interview I made one comment to the superintendent that got me in. I said, 'I think we're in show business.' He said, 'That's what I wanted to hear.' I went home and told my wife, 'I think I'm going to get that job.' "

Anderson High was the only school in town for three-quarters of a century, until the mid-fifties, when Highland High was annexed into the city of Anderson and Madison Heights High was created to educate the sons and daughters of an expanding GM management. Although the Indians didn't exactly warm to the prospect of competition, the threat seemed harmless enough, for Anderson High still had the most students.

A decade later, the civil rights movement changed all that. School districts were redrawn, the most dramatic change splitting a large, predominantly black neighborhood, the source of many of Anderson's best players, almost in half. Students living south of 22nd Street were assigned to Madison Heights; north of 22nd Street, to Anderson. Still other residents were bused to Highland, and for the first time there was real, serious competition in Anderson.

Most Hoosiers now rate the Anderson sectional as the toughest of all the sixty-four sectional tournaments. Sectional week is the most passionate time of the year, a few days in mid-February when three Anderson schools and five smaller local schools go hand-to-hand for the right of only one to survive to the regional round. Hostilities simmer within acceptable limits throughout most of the year, but at sectional time Anderson takes on a little breath of Ulster.

It was only a generation ago that everyone in town went to Anderson High, so there are many families with parents who bleed red and green and kids who go to Madison Heights or Highland. Detente is fragile in these interfaith households; during sectional week there are a lot of scraping chairs and unfinished meals.

"My daughter was a cheerleader at Anderson High, and so was her best friend," recalls Brenda Weinzaphel, treasurer of the Anderson High Booster's Club. "But her friend's mother was a secretary at Madison Heights and her dad taught at Highland. She'd get into it all the time with her parents. Finally it got so bad she had to come to stay at our house during sectional week."

The tension seems to grip adults harder than kids, who get to mix at parties and in back seats and on outdoor courts. But much of Anderson's service club life revolves around basketball in the winter, and it is harder for adults—especially Old Indians, who still regard the other two schools as bratty newcomers—to forgive and forget. There are those who will not shop in rival neighborhoods.

On a summer evening in the Olympia Lounge—an Indian stronghold, a place to catch the Celtics on cable when the Indians aren't playing in the winter and to take in a wet T-shirt contest in the summer—the wife of a dentist, a diehard Indian who says her husband thinks she is crazy to care so much, is happy to lay out the turf.

"We get along better with the Madison Heights people than the Highland people," she says. "The Highland people are conniving. I know so much about them that most people don't know. Their coach will go out to this place on 38th Street where everyone plays in the summertime and get real chummy with 'em. He tries to talk kids into going to Highland, into living with somebody else in the Highland area. Two of our players moved to Highland. Norm thinks it cost us a state championship. And Norm gave their coach his first job."

Madison Heights rates a little better, even for a "Bobby Knight school." In the Olympia Lounge, Madison Heights coach Phil Buck—an Indiana University alum—is branded as a clone of Knight, the Indiana University coach, while Held is admired as a maverick, one who won't imitate Knight's vaunted "motion offense" and slow the game down to, as Held puts it, "eleven passes and a shot."

A lot of this seems to be a reaction to Knight's not having recruited Troy Lewis, Anderson High's star and one of the two best players in the state. It is said that Indiana University never even sent Troy a letter. In the Olympia, Buck is suspected of discouraging Knight from pursuing Lewis. It is furthermore taken as an article of faith that so pointed a snub could only have been Knight's way of warning Norm Held to toe the line.

Held is asked about the rivalry with Highland and Madison Heights. "The ambition of every young person in this whole area," he says, "is to beat the Indians. People would rather beat us than eat. They'd give up eating for a whole week to beat us. When I look at the other two schools in town, hey, they've got good basketball programs, but . . . not quite the Indians. Everybody knows that. Most of the parents of those kids played in the Wigwam for the Indians. They want our tradition and they're gaining on us. Maybe someday they'll get there."

Susan Held, a direct, attractive woman who enjoys teaching fifth grade, has been with Norm since he started coaching. Sometimes she finds herself thinking back to the small Illinois towns: "There just wasn't the pressure that you find in Anderson," she says. "It's the three schools that make

The maiden and the brave stare down Anderson's opponents during pregame warmups. *(John E. Simon)* (**LEFT**)

Elders of the tribe at home in the Wigwam. *(Norm Johnston)*

One of the faceless masses exhorts the red and green.

(Dale Pickett)

Mary Anderson High players find college crowds a let-down after the supercharged atmosphere of the Wigwam.

(John E. Simon)

Friday night fever: 9,000 fans attend a home game at Anderson High. *(Norm Johnston)*

Anderson's Norm Held: "I think we're in show business." *(John E. Simon)* (RIGHT)

it really tough. In other towns, everybody's been behind you, there haven't been all these factions against you built in right from the start. Here, no matter what you do, you have these people from the other schools who are against you.

"I always hear comments about how calm I am at the games, but it's all inside of me." Several years ago, after she heard her neighbors booing their son during a game, she moved to the front row of the Wigwam, around a corner and maybe twenty feet from Norm. During the action, tension forces her lips into a thin straight line. Like Norm, her legs are clamped together at the thighs. While Norm wrings a red handkerchief, Susan smoothes her program on her lap, occasionally restoring her hands to a prayerful position.

She has become accustomed, if not resigned, to life as the first lady of Redbud City. When, after an evening of dancing at the new Interstate Sheraton, midnight passes and Norm cannot seem to pull away from the fiftieth quartet of fans wanting to know about Troy Lewis or the Connersville game, Susan simply kicks off her heels and stretches out on a couch. "When we go to a restaurant, everybody will turn and look," she says. "I guess Norm is a celebrity here. It feels like every move you make is being watched. . . . I think I've gotten worse about it as I've gotten older. Twelve or thirteen years ago Norm quit [coaching] for a year and he went into this deep depression. I can take it until he's ready."

An hour before game time, the fragrance of fresh popcorn already fills the Wigwam. The Indian boosters are busy at their table, unboxing high school basketball's most complete product line. Tonight's assortment includes Wigwam postcards, a poster of the team in headdresses and on horseback (last year's poster had them on motorcycles as "Held's Angels"), cushions, embroidered Indian heads, "We're Number One" mittens, license plates, window decals, Indian statues, men's ties and women's ties, "Anything that's red and green," says a smiling booster.

At the press table, technicians wearing headphones are checking their leads. The floor below is a tangle of wire; WLHM, WAXT and HBU will all broadcast tonight's game. It will be televised on local cable, and Channel 6 is here, too, for spot coverage back to Indianapolis. It seems impossible that this is a high school game.

After a while, fans start to trickle, then flow, then surge into the gym. Young families, guys in ballcaps, arrive first to begin their long trek upstairs to aeries that call for keen eyes. Then older, nicely dressed quartets, the boys steering the girls with a light touch on the back, dawdle momentarily at courtside to watch layup drills and then finally sift into the top and middle seats of the floor level. Everyone seems to know everyone else.

Just below them, arriving fashionably late, are the town's gentry, including Mayor McMahan, members of the school board and the managerial elite. One of them turns out to be Carl Erskine, class of '45. The old Dodger curveballer is today president of the First National Bank of Madison County.

Erskine swears he is remembered locally as a set-shooter rather than a Giant-killer. "Hardly a day goes by when somebody doesn't stop me on the street and say 'Carl, hey, uh, remember that game when you . . .' and I think they're gonna talk about the Yankees. Then they'll say, 'I was in the old Wigwam that day you made that one from the corner against Kokomo.' Here, I'm not a Dodger, I'm an Indian."

As tipoff time draws near, the opposing cheerleaders are squatting around the center circle, passing a peace pipe. Suddenly the lights go out. Everyone leaps to their feet, whooping in the dark as the Wigwam reels with the thunder of tom-toms. All at once a spotlight falls upon an Indian brave in full headdress, arms folded across his bare chest.

He dances in wide circles around the gym, then cuts abruptly into the center circle as the spotlight broadens. There, kneeling, is a maiden. The crowd noise would mute the Concorde. As the two hold a long, unblinking stare, she rises and they begin to dance slowly together, mingling rather sensually for high school fare in central Indiana. He bolts loose for a final circle, breaks in again and leaps over her. They stride from the spotlight together and the crowd cuts loose with one last great whoop.

The Dance of the Brave and the Maiden is a sacred tradition in Anderson, maybe fifty years old. Competition for the roles of the brave and the maiden is said to be as keen as that for starting forward on the team. The dance is believed to have an intimidating effect on the opponents, some of whom remain in the locker room until it is done. Held, for one, believes the dance has won some games for the Indians, although he thinks occasionally it backfires by stimulating opponents to unnatural heights.

Because the ceremony of the game means almost as much here as its playing, cheerleaders, majorettes, band members and dancers have long been respected at Anderson as they are in few other places. "I was a cheerleader at New Castle High," recalls Brenda Weinzaphel, "and to come to Anderson and see the maiden and the brave dance and pass the pipe, that was the high point of the year. At Anderson High a cheerleader really means something. When my daughter made cheerleader here, I was in ecstasy."

28

* * *

The lights come back on, and, when vision and hearing are again possible, a neighbor points out that all that the best seats in the house are occupied by very old people, mainly, it turns out, by members of seventeen families who have held season tickets for over fifty years, along with the interlopers who sat down thirty or forty years ago.

Season tickets for those seats are Anderson's crown jewels. You work your way down toward them row by row, year by year throughout the course of your life. At the Wigwam you begin at the top and descend when someone dies or moves away or forgets to renew. The players get closer as your ability to see them gets worse. From the young families up in the clouds down to the gerentocracy at courtside, Anderson's human geology is recorded in the strata of the Wigwam.

Word that one of these tickets has become available is whispered among family members and trusted friends, like word of a vacant rent-controlled apartment in Manhattan. These tickets surface from time to time in wills, and Indian ticket manager Jack Macy has three times been summoned to testify as to their proper custody in spiteful divorce hearings.

Dan Quickel, 81, has what seems to be the best seat in the house, front row center. He is happy to share the story of his marvelous descent. "I started out in the top of the old Wigwam in the student section," he recalls. "I bought my first season ticket in 1928, when I was a freshman. I had to sit with the students until I graduated in 1931." When he came home from Cornell and law school at the University of Michigan, opportunity knocked, hard. Waiting was the break of a lifetime.

"My father had become team physician. Because of that, he could get us into all the games, row three." From there it was all downhill, so to speak. "Then we were in the second row when the new gym opened. We had three seats together. Then Father died at the age of ninety-nine. He was getting ready to go to the ball game when he fell down the stairs and couldn't come anymore. After that Charlie Cummins, the athletic director, put us in the first row, section D, down by the stage. Finally, two seats opened up front row center, and we were delighted to take them."

In 1983–84, the Indiana High School Athletic Association allotted Anderson High School 1,800 sectional tournament tickets to distribute to 5,875 season ticket holders. The students, staff and faculty claimed over a thousand, leaving 654 for 4,000 hopefuls.

Like most Indiana schools, the Indians hold a drawing to distribute tournament tickets. "Lottery Night" has become such a great party that Indian fans look forward to it almost as much as the games. To enter, you hand in your regular season ticket stub one weekday before the sectional—during Red and Green Week, when everything in town looks like a Christmas package—and then return to the Wigwam at eight that night for the drawing.

Actually, you could show up at 8:00 for the drawing, because it is preceded by at least an hour of speeches and fight songs and syncopated cheers. Each team member gets to shuffle up to the mike amid riotous applause for a few defiant words, and the booster product line appears once more.

Finally, one blindfolded student cranks the drum and another yells out a number. There's a shriek and a woman in a red blouse and a green skirt bounds down the stairs to claim her tourney ticket. For more than an hour down they come, in every combination of red and green, until the drum is empty.

Although Jack Macy insists he's never been offered a bribe for a tourney ticket, that doesn't mean every rabid Indian fan is content to trust the tournament to blindfolded students. Ron Porter remembers scoring eight tickets for the state finals one year by stapling six season ticket stubs from the previous year to his two current tickets, and then getting lucky in the drawing: "And then I was walkin' out of the gym and a guy said, 'R.P., I'll give you a hundred dollars apiece for 'em.' I said, 'No way, no way.'"

Though Anderson High celebrates the game ritually and in multitudes, though the flock has at least once passed the hat to erect a truly flattering place of worship, though the prayers are earnest and the faith unbroken—the gods have not smiled on the Indians since 1946. Since then, the Indians have escaped their wicked sectional—which surely can be likened to the valley of the shadow of death—many times, captured regional and semistate crowns and have reached the final, *final* game for the championship of all 400 Hoosier schools, three times in the last seven years—only to lose by four points, and then two and finally *one* excruciating point—and what do they have to show for it? Tears. Bring on the locusts and frogs and boils. Enough of this.

"We're snakebit," says Ron Porter. "There's no other way to explain it. Year after year we have the statistics, the superstars, and something always happens." Porter can tell the story firsthand, for no matter where he has been or what has been going on in his life, he has been with the Indians in spirit or flesh every year since his graduation in

1962—and he has even made a little spending money on the side. A sampling of Ron Porter's postgraduate years leaves no room for doubt about the intensity of his faith:

"In '68–'69 I was at the top of the gym when we got beat by Highland in the sectional. We were down by one point with about forty-four seconds to go, and Artie Pepelea—runs an insurance agency with Norm now—shot a shot from the ten-second line that went over the backboard and into the stage. I just went wild. I was so mad I left my ex-wife at the gym. I was screamin' and cussin' and stomped down those stairs and out of the gym and got in my car and drove to my buddy's house and got drunk. It was one of those days.

"In '73–'74 we were 27–0, ranked fifth in the *nation* by some magazine. We had to play in the Fort Wayne semistate. I went up to northern Indiana and bought 500 tickets from the different schools in the semistate. Me and four other guys, we left Anderson at midnight and drove to Elkhart and bought 150 tickets for four dollars apiece and I was sellin' 'em for twenty. That night we played Fort Wayne Northrup and we lost. Unbelievable.

"Let's see, '79 is when I thought I had the heart attack. We were in the state finals and this girl and I were drivin' to Indianapolis for the afternoon game. I was workin' for Stupes Buick and I made him give me a light-green-and-dark-green Regal to drive to the game. Then I started havin' chest pains. She had to drive me back to the hospital. I'm missin' the game, I'm pissed so I make 'em put it on the radio in the emergency room. Then the guy comes in and says, 'There's nothin' wrong with you, but tonight I want you to come in and get an upper GI.' We beat Argos in the afternoon and so I just got dressed and drove to Indianapolis. I went to Steak and Ale, had dinner, went to the finals and we got beat."

But *the* game, the one that sent Porter and nearly every other Indian fan combing back through the collective past for trace of some unpaid karmic debt—like, maybe somebody really *did* burn down the first Wigwam—was the one-point loss to Connersville for the 1983 state title. The game boiled down to one shot, a shot that Troy Lewis took from eighteen feet.

In ten years at Anderson, Norm Held's teams have won about 75 percent of their games and gone to the state finals three times. Held is one of the most successful coaches in Indiana, but the final seconds of the Connersville game remain hauntingly clear: Behind by one point, the Indians took the ball downcourt and held it for about thirty-five seconds. With three seconds left, Lewis dribbled it into the middle and shot a jumper. Held thought all his trials were over. "The ball looked dead-center, but it hit the front of the rim and bounced up and off . . . it just didn't go in."

Ron Porter was listening to the game by telephone from Houston with his roommate, Ron James. "I just went numb. My roommate was on the phone at the end, I couldn't take it. With about thirty seconds left, he says to me, 'Listen, I can't stand this, Norm's holdin' the ball for the last shot.' When Lewis missed, I just went numb. We were bigger than them, we could've gone inside and got fouled or got a last-second shot . . . I couldn't believe it."

Brenda Weinzaphel was stricken. "I cried all the way home. My husband didn't know what to do with me. When that shot didn't go in, I went into the lobby at Market Square, and I don't even remember being out there. I cried all the next day. Even today, I can be in the car driving, I can think about it and I'll be there again. It hurts."

Susan Held remembers waking up the following morning. "The very first thought I had was, 'Something is wrong.

Something terrible has happened.' Then, when you finally
realize what it is, you think, 'Oh, no, it really did happen.'
It took me days and weeks and maybe months to get over
such a loss. It was like a death. I would've stayed in if it
weren't for my husband. I'm not as good as he is at getting
over losses."

Troy Lewis is an open, soft-spoken and appealing young
man now attending Purdue. He was still dreaming about
the shot the following summer: "My goal growing up was
to win the state championship. I used to watch it on TV all
the time when I was little. I'd have this feeling, you know,
man, this is great, I'd do anything just to play in this . . .
I always dreamed about hittin' the last-second shot. Then
I had my chance and I missed it. Now I dream that I'm
shootin' the shot but then something else happens and I
don't have to shoot it."

The memory of a game like that dies hard in Anderson,
Indiana, but the years have taken the sting out of four other
final game losses, and this too will pass. For the willing,
there is comfort to be found in the view of Dan Quickel,
an elder of the tribe who was watching money shots spin
in and out with Lewis's grandfather and Porter's dad.

Asked if the Connersville game was a particularly bitter
pill to swallow, Quickel smiles. "No, no, all the games have
been marvelous, every one of them has been good . . . you
know, I've lived in the same house now forty-four years
and just last year a young couple moved in next door—
couldn't be older than 25. They have two little kids. Now
every game my wife and I see them at the Wigwam, way
up where I started out. It makes you feel good. Basketball
is just a way of life here."

FARM BOYS

"Round my Indiana Homestead" (as they sang in years gone by)
Now the basketballs are flying and they almost hide the sky;
For each gym is full of players and each town is full of gyms
As a hundred thousand snipers shoot their goals with deadly glims

Old New York may have its subway with its famous Rum Row trust
And old Finland with its Nurm runs our runners into dust
But where candlelights are gleaming through the sycamores afar
Every son of Indiana shoots his basket like a star.
—GRANTLAND RICE,
"Back in 1925"

It's not easy to swallow, but the cold fact is that basketball didn't start in Indiana. It should have, but it didn't. It has taken Bobby Knight to find a way out: "Basketball may have been invented in Massachusetts," he said in 1984, "but it was made *for* Indiana."

The vector of "Hoosier Hysteria" has been identified as the Reverend Nicholas McKay, a Presbyterian minister born in England. In 1893 McKay was assigned to a YMCA in Crawfordsville, Indiana. En route, he visited Dr. James Naismith's YMCA camp in Springfield, Massachusetts, where basketball had been invented two years before.

McKay gave it mixed reviews. It was active enough to occupy rugby—er, football—players in the winter, but he could see it needed polishing. After all, it was only dumbest luck that they weren't all playing "boxball." Naismith had told the janitor to bring up a couple of boxes, but all the bloke had been able to find were peach baskets. Then they had nailed the baskets to a balcony railing and moved a stepladder under each basket. After every goal someone had to climb up and toss down the ball.

After Reverend McKay started his own YMCA in Crawfordsville—above a tavern—he hired a blacksmith to forge two metal hoops, sewed coffee sacks around them and nailed them to the walls. Having gone so far as to eliminate the stepladder—and "ladder-obstructed" tickets—McKay left a few glitches for the centuries to iron out. "Being just about the tallest and slimmest kid on the floor," wrote Dr. James B. Griffith, who played in McKay's first organized game, "it became my job, right off, to jump up each time a goal was made and knock the ball out of the sack . . . the thing I remember most vividly is having a pair of bruised knuckles next morning."

Basketball was indeed made for Indiana. It was a game to play in the winter, something between harvest and planting, something to do besides euchre and the lodge and church and repairing equipment. At the turn of the century, when Indiana was a landscape mainly of small towns and crossroads hamlets—settlements of a few houses, a church, a schoolhouse and maybe a lodge—basketball was a godsend.

Most towns were too small to find enough guys for a football team and too poor to buy all the pads and helmets. But it was easy enough to nail a hoop to a pole or a barn, and you could just shoot around by yourself if there wasn't anybody else, just to see how many in a row you could make.

Basketball was epidemic in Indiana within a year after McKay carried it in. In Madison, they played in the skating rink; in Carmel, in the driveway of a lumber yard, with spectators hooting from atop skids of walnut. Other towns shoved the pews against the church walls or dragged the desks from the schoolhouses out into the snow.

Rules, such as they were, were highly customized. The town of Amboy surrounded its court with chicken wire, so that the ball would always be in play. In Clinton, they liked to bank the ball in off the ceiling. Brawls were common, and in the Dodge City days, an athletic supporter was someone who came to watch you play.

Each March since 1911, Hoosier schoolboys have played in the State High School Basketball Tournament. The first "tourney," as it has always been called, was sponsored by the Indiana University Booster's Club, who viewed the occasion as a chance to recruit players away from Purdue and Notre Dame.

The boosters invited each of Indiana's thirteen congressional districts to send its best team to Bloomington, no questions asked. Usually, local play made it clear who was best, but sometimes there were mitigating circumstances. For example, South Bend High School informed the boosters that Rochester High had compiled a better record in season play only because one of their forwards was really a Notre Dame student who came home on weekends. The boosters held themselves above this ugliness, perhaps because they knew that the boy, Hugh Barnhart, was also the son of the local congressman.

When the news reached Crawfordsville that their own Athenians had won the first tourney, the town went bonkers. Citizens tore shouting through the streets, men with their coats turned inside out. Church bells tolled throughout the town. They danced around a mighty bonfire until someone heard the train whistle. Then they all sprinted to meet the Monon, steaming in from Bloomington. Only thing was, the players weren't on the train. Exhausted, they had spent the night in Bloomington.

Indiana's first superstar was a plowboy named Homer Stonebreaker. He played in 1913 and 1914 for Wingate High School, a crossroads schoolhouse whose enrollment included only twelve boys. Like many Hoosier schools at the time, Wingate High was a room with a stove, a place in out of the cold where a few kids might learn something useful until the ground could take a plow. Having no gym, they practiced outside, except for the one evening a week when Coach Jesse Wood hitched up a team and cantered six miles to a gym at New Richmond.

"Stoney," as he was called, was a 6'4" center who wouldn't have given ground to a gorilla under the boards. He scored most of his points by squatting quickly and spinning up long, looping underhand shots. It is said that opposing coaches ordered their players to pick up Stoney at midcourt, but often even that was too late.

In Bloomington, the Wingate players were less than unheralded; they were ridiculed. Indeed they must have looked a little out of it. While everyone else wore monogrammed tank tops and short pants, the Wingate boys took to the court in sweatshirts, baseball pants and long socks.

But they COULD play. Wingate won four games—only one of them close—and then faced South Bend High School for the state championship. The game was a gem; Wingate won on a shot by forward Forest Crane late in the fifth overtime period.

Stoney and the "Gymless Wonders," as they were called, were instant folk heroes. Challenges came from all over the state the next season. They were happy to oblige. Great convoys of Model Ts formed in the town square, and out they rumbled. Five hundred fans chartered a train for the Kokomo game.

Wingate repeated as champions in 1914, with Stoney scoring all of Wingate's seventeen points in the closest game, against Clinton. Not many are left who saw him—coach Wood outlived all his players and is now in his 90s—but Stoney's memory shines bright. "I used to ask the old-timers if there were any players from the early days who could still play today," says Bob Collins, sports editor of the Indianapolis *Star*. "Three names usually came out: Johnny Wooden, Fuzzy Vandervier [who led Franklin High School to three consecutive championships] and Homer Stonebreaker."

*   *   *

To cope with the tourney's explosive growth—entries increased twentyfold in the first ten years—officials in 1915 broke the tourney into local eliminations called "sectionals," whose winners met for the state championship.

Nostrils flared at once. With local bragging rights at stake, sectional games became mythic events, battlegrounds where martyrs fell. Losses were seeping wounds that festered in coffee shops all summer long.

The sectionals were organized basically at the county level, and in Indiana counties amounted to several hamlets connected by pure rancor to the local Kremlin, the county seat. The litany of complaints against the county seat became a part of Indiana's special script, as even and soothing as a chorus of locusts on a summer night. It was common knowledge in the provinces that the school in the county seat typically had the following advantages:

1. The home court in the sectional.
2. An amoral coach.
3. A county all-star team, full of kids who should have been going to other schools.
4. A pair of forwards who had voted in the last election.
5. A center in his third year as a junior.
6. A network of grade schools that would shame the Yankees' farm system.

Winning was everything; amateurism was a sick joke. Merchants rewarded winning coaches with bonuses—once a Pontiac sedan—and kids with gold watches. Coaches went after the parents of any tall kid who could shoot a lick, promising a better job in their town.

"It was just dog eat dog," says Phil Eskew, 80, former commissioner of the Indiana High School Athletic Association (IHSAA). "The basketball players were important kids in anybody's town, and they could go anywhere they wanted. There were married and overaged kids playin' kids that hadn't passed a subject."

The minutes of the early years of the IHSAA, which began in 1903 as a posse of school administrators determined to regulate high school sports, read like a police docket: damage claims for broken windows, referees assaulted, fights, illegal rewards and more fights. One letter from Anderson High accuses rival Cicero High of "re-oiling" its players in a 1916 contest. Unfortunately, the author did not describe the crime, nor did he explain why the original "oiling" went unchallenged.

In 1916, the IHSAA hired a lawman, Arthur L. Trester, the tough, uncompromising son of Quaker parents, and gave him a free hand. At once, he set about straightening out the books and making eligibility rules for players and teams. The challenge would be making them stick. Square-jawed, 6'4" and powerfully built, Arthur Trester was not the blinking kind.

Overnight, Trester's office became the state's woodshed. When you were accused of something, you got a letter from Trester, had the trip to Indianapolis to think about it and felt your heart against your ribs as the elevator carried you to the eighth floor of the Circle Tower Building. Lips dry, you stated you case. Trester would listen and make his ruling. There was no appeal. "The rules are clear, the penalties severe," he would say to those who sought a discussion.

Charles O. Finley, who, as the owner of the Oakland Athletics baseball team, seemed to enjoy testing the power of the commissioner's office, cut his teeth as a student on Arthur Trester's IHSAA. When he was accused of enrolling

42

in a Gary high school to play a sport without changing residence, he was summoned to Circle Tower. Trester heard him out and banned Finley from competition for a year. The rule was clear, the penalty severe.

Trester lived by his own rules. When a member of his IHSAA Board of Control—or "Board of Controlled," as the press termed it—dared to light a cigarette at a meeting, Trester would throw the window open and pretend to gag. "He would have liked to have broken down and had some fun," says Phil Eskew, "but he couldn't. He made the rules."

Again and again the state legislature tried to take over the IHSAA and its huge booty of basketball revenue. It galled the lawmakers that they could not deliver tourney tickets to their constituents. When the challenges came, Trester would stay up all night, organizing coaches and principals to come to Indianapolis for "their" association. Trester sat silently through hearings, letting others defend him against charges of greed and gross megalomania. Then, when the bell rang, he got up and the lawmakers scrambled after him, begging for just four, even *two* tickets.

Trester was even the chief referee. In the 1932 Muncie regional tournament, with Muncie Central leading New Castle by one point, a New Castle guard named Vernon Huffman heaved the ball toward the basket from midcourt at the buzzer.

Unbelievably, the ball swished through the basket, but one official was signaling that the basket had counted and the other was gesturing no basket. As fans poured onto the floor, the referees plunged into the dressing room and pushed the door shut.

Soon they agreed, but there was no way they were going to announce their decision before talking to Trester; he signed the cards that *made* them referees. They called him again and again. No answer. So they drove off to Yorktown for a bite, leaving thousands in anguish. At six that evening Trester returned the call, listened to the story and told the officials he would back their decisions against the storm that would surely come. Not until then did the two men announce New Castle's victory.

In 1925 Dr. James Naismith, the inventor of the game, visited the Indiana state finals as Trester's guest. They sat among 15,000 screaming fans and watched a superb game. Naismith was stunned. He could not believe what had happened to the diversion he had started with two peach baskets. "The possibilities of basketball as seen there were a revelation to me," he wrote when he returned home.

Until Henry Ford ruined everything, Hoosier engineers dominated the American auto industry. At least 375 models have been made in Indiana, most of them in the first third of the century. Spring would come, and the tinkerers would push back their shop doors and roll out elegant custom touring cars like the National, with its push-button electric gearshift, the Cole, with its revolutionary V-8 engine, and the Waverly, darling of the ladies with veils and linen dusters.

Unlike the other mainly midwestern states where basketball came to dominate small-town life in the early part of the century, Indiana was relatively easy to get around. Hoosierland is small and mainly flat, and its early roads were built to carry and test the great roadsters. When the cars became powerful enough, a statewide newspaper, the Indianapolis *News*, emerged. One barnstorming reporter, William Fox, Jr., set out to bring the tourney to every Hoosier.

Each year between 1928 and 1936, Fox, together with Butler University coach Tony Hinkle, leaped into a donated Stutz Bearcat at the final buzzer of the Indianapolis regional afternoon game, shot up to Muncie for the evening final and tried to make it all the way to Fort Wayne for their tourney celebration.

After that they had three days to criss-cross the state from Lake Michigan to the Ohio River in order to make Fox's deadline. Hinkle drove by day and Fox wrote by night; they rarely saw each other awake. But it worked. "Shootin' 'Em and Stoppin' 'Em" became every Hoosier's column. Fox's turgid dispatches from the sixteen fronts gave those whose world view ended at the county line a surpassing knowledge of statewide geography.

Unlike its neighbors, Hoosierland had no major-league franchises to distract from its obsession. Illinois was the Chicago Cubs and Bears and White Sox, Ohio the Cleveland Browns and Indians and Cincinnati Reds, Michigan the Detroit Lions and Tigers. Indiana was the Frankfort Hot Dogs, the Vincennes Alices, the Delphi Oracles and the Martinsville Artesians.

Fox magnified local heroics into mythical events. Players and coaches achieved almost scriptural stature. Johnny Wooden, who played three years in the state finals, probably came to mean more to a kid in Indiana than Ty Cobb to a kid in Michigan. "Wooden, to the kids of my generation, was what Bill Russell, Wilt Chamberlain and Lew Alcindor were years later," broadcaster Tommy Harmon has said. "He was king, the idol of every kid who had a basketball. In Indiana, that was *every* kid."

Fox's gravel-filled accounts and predictions became so popular that the *News*' chief rival, the Indianapolis *Times*, hired an airplane to race Hinkle and Fox around Indiana.

45

"Don't take basketball season or life too seriously," advised Fox in one column, perhaps thinking about the increased weight of Hinkle's foot on the pedal as he glanced nervously toward the heavens. "Both are too short."

While New York City tried to scrape the skies with office buildings of Hoosier limestone, back home they piled it up against the schoolhouse. Even small towns built gyms that could hold everyone around, for everyone went to the games.

"I've been in places where I was having dinner on Friday night," says Bob Collins, "and the owner would shout, 'Fifteen minutes and we're closin' up!' and everybody cleaned their plates, settled up and went to the basketball game."

Friday night was the perfect time to rob a small-town Indiana bank. "The game was the only activity in town," says Collins. "They had the bake sale at the gym, and the mothers conducted their raffle. I remember one time I went to a game in a place called Grass Creek and watched a kid play tuba in the band. Then he showed up in the reserve game a few minutes later, still dripping wet from his shower after the band quit playing."

"These gyms are our nightclubs," explained Fox to the nation in the *Saturday Evening Post*, "and we don't have to import any Billy Roses to put on our shows. At any ordinary high school game you will see bedizened and be-dimpled drum majorettes leading bands through intricate formations before they toss their batons over the baskets in big league football game fashion. Our floor shows are second to none."

Along with the standard two- to three-thousand-seaters

in little towns, genuine monsters began to shadow the snowscape as well, facilities bigger than all but a few college gyms. The incentive was simple: the team with the biggest gym got to host the sectional. As sectionals were added, Hoosierland erupted into gym wars, with communities emptying their building funds and floating bonds to finance bigger and bigger gyms.

"No distinctions divide the crowds which pack the school gymnasium for home games and which in every kind of machine crowd the roads for out-of-town games," wrote sociologists Warren and Helen Lynd of Muncie in 1929. "North Side and South Side, Catholic and Kluxer, banker and machinist—their one shout is 'Eat 'em, beat 'em Bearcats!' "

During a 1929 meeting in which a motion to put up an extra $300 to hire a librarian was voted down, the Muncie City Council decided to reward Muncie Central's 1928 champs by spending $100,000 for what was to be the "biggest gym in America." Today, with its 7,400 seats, it is surpassed only by seven gyms in Indiana and one in Texas.

Other Indiana communities turned the Great Depression to their advantage. President Franklin D. Roosevelt created the Works Project Administration—or, as many Hoosiers called it, "We Piddle Around"—as a way to get America's laborers back on their feet by giving them things to build. "I attended grade school in Spurgeon, that's eight miles south of Winslow," says Eugene Cato, the current IHSAA commissioner. "I can remember we'd go outside on the playground to play basketball and these gentlemen would be working on the gym. A lot of them were black, and I doubt if we had a black in Pike County."

F.D.R. may have had roads and sidewalks and bridges

in mind, but Hoosier politicians knew what was essential. Hell, you could always build a road.

In 1930 the first black player appeared on a tourney championship team. His name was Dave Dejernette. It would have been Dave Miller, except that at the age of 16 his grandfather had been sold from one slavemaster named Miller to another named Dejernette.

Dave's father, John, was a strapping man, a railroad worker who had grown up in rural Kentucky. "One day in 1913 a white man came through offering twelve cents an hour for good colored workers," says Dave's younger brother Basil. They wanted men who would pick up and help dig the B&O railroad out from a flood. John went with him and the next spring came back for his wife Mary and their two young children. They moved to Washington, Indiana.

David Dejernette, the third of John and Mary's six children, grew up at a time when there were still two kinds of Hoosier hysteria: on hot summer nights the Dejernettes would see their white neighbors walk out of their houses and into the night with sheets over their heads.

At times it was a dangerous place for Washington's few black families, the Harmons and the Ballous, the Cotts and the Johnsons and the Dejernettes. Most blacks lived in a small neighborhood on the west side of town. There they had their own small Methodist church, with Mary as pastor. John made a point to talk clearly to the children about how to handle themselves in town and at school.

"He told us always to be respectful," says Basil Dejernette. "He said, keep to your books and learn everything you can. And don't go making wisecracks. But he said, don't let anyone hurt you, either. If someone tries to hurt you, stand your ground."

Dave Dejernette would have stood his ground pretty well. He grew to be 6'4½" in high school and weighed 225 pounds. He was a fast runner and an overpowering rebounder. He became the dominant basketball player in Indiana.

The week before the 1930 tourney, Washington was to play Vincennes High School, whose team Washington had already beaten twice that season. A few days before the game a letter arrived at the school, addressed to Dave. It was a death threat warning him not to play against Vincennes and signed "the KKK." Dave took the letter home to his parents.

That evening his coach, Burl Friddle, walked out to the Dejernette home. John appeared at the door. "You going to let John go to Vincennes?" Friddle asked. "No, I don't think he'd be safe," John Dejernette replied. "You let him go and I'll protect him," said Friddle. "How?" "I'll see that he's protected." According to Basil, it took Friddle most of the night to convince John, and John until dawn to convince Mary. The next morning John told Friddle that Dave could go, but he was going too.

John took a pistol to Vincennes and watched closely from the bleachers. There was no attempt on Dave, although during the game there was a shock in the bleachers when an overwrought fan died suddenly of a heart attack. When John and Dave got home, Mary was waiting up. Shocked, she saw John remove the gun from his coat. "What happened?" she asked, eyes wide. "Well," said John, unable to resist, "a man died in Vincennes tonight."

*   *   *

Like enchanted stock, the tourney kept growing and splitting through the Great War and the Great Depression, adding sectionals and more weekend rounds—called regionals and semistates—as more and more schools entered. For the country schoolhouses, the regionals and semistates expanded the universe. To play a game before a multitude in a great house in Fort Wayne or Evansville, with the press corps taking up one end of the court, was like a field trip to a foreign capital. The new rounds gave the big schools a chance to dress up and look their best.

Nothing could dilute the demand for tickets. Tickets for the 1940 Kokomo regional were to go on sale at the school on March 12 at 7:00 A.M. The first customer appeared at 5:30 the afternoon before. By midnight there were 600 in line. They made blanket tents and tried to deal cards around kerosene heaters. Enterprising kids shuttled coffee and short-order meals to the supplicants. At 4:00 A.M., police, fearing a riot, forced school officials to open the ticket windows. All the tickets were gone in a half-hour.

Despite the odds against the little schools, Hoosiers did not divide the tourney into classes by enrollment, like most other states, when the tournament became unwieldy. The tourney had become a perfect metaphor for the Hoosier outlook: it gave everyone a chance but no one a handout.

In 1928 Butler University, a small college known for its pharmaceutical program, built America's largest basketball field house, seating 15,000, to give Arthur Trester a home for the state finals. Trester gave Butler $100,000 for ten years' rent. "We sure never had any trouble building a great schedule," laughs Tony Hinkle, Butler's coach at the time. "Teams would come through from the west, headed for Madison Square Garden, but they always wanted to stop here, just to play in this building."

The finals were held in Butler Field House—now re-named for Hinkle—until 1971. It is hard to imagine a building that has meant more to Indiana, or a better place to watch a basketball game. In the afternoon, the sun pours down through mammoth windows onto the polished floor. The seats are painted in bright primary colors. There is not a column in the place. "When other schools started building field houses, architects used to come in here all the time," says Hinkle. "They said they liked the way the space flowed out."

A ticket to vintage "Hoosier Hysteria"—as Fox called the tourney—was a pass to the "Sweet Sixteen." Between 1921 and 1936, the winners of sixteen regional tournaments met in a dawn-till-midnight two-day elimination to decide the state champion. It was like a marathon dance. Teams that made the Sweet Sixteen were said by Fox to pass through the "Pearly Gates of Butler Field House"; those that survived probably felt ready to meet their Maker.

Almost all the tickets went to the high schools of Indiana, who honored their best senior athletes with a trip to In-dianapolis. When the sunlight struck their brilliant letter sweaters, the bleachers blazed with color, like autumn in Vermont. "Ah, it was just a *beautiful* sight," says Hinkle.

Herb Schwomeyer, 70, known throughout Indiana as the "Hoosier Hysteria Historian" saw the first of his fifty-four consecutive state finals—a Sweet Sixteen—as a high school junior in 1932. "That Friday was the only day in my whole school career that my parents ever let me miss school with-out being sick," Schwomeyer says, smiling at the memory. "My dad bought that ticket for me for three dollars—that's three dollars for fifteen games, Friday and Saturday. He gave me three more dollars and told me to buy a ticket for him for Saturday if I could.

"So my mother packed a big twenty-pound grocery sack full of lunch for me and I went out. At eight-thirty in the morning Vincennes, which was highly favored, got upset by Cicero. Soon as the game ended I went down to Gate three to try to buy a ticket for my dad. The Vincennes fans were already going back home. I was able to buy twelve tickets for a quarter apiece, and another two people *gave* me their tickets.

"I saved the best ticket for my dad and at noon I went outside and sold thirteen tickets for three dollars apiece. That's thirty-nine bucks." Schwomeyer, in the telling, still seems to be marveling at such a fortune. "That's more money than I had ever had in my life. I remember I went back in and watched the rest of the games with my hand in my pocket so the money wouldn't get stolen. I haven't missed a tourney since."

"People would hide in here the day before," says Hinkle, gesturing toward the upper reaches of the great room. "We'd have to have the police come in and sweep the field house. Once I caught a guy climbing up a drainpipe toward a window. I said, 'What are you doing up there?' and he said, 'Oh, just trying to see if I could make it.'

"I remember once telling Arthur Trester, 'If you want, I'll put in another five thousand seats for you at two dollars per seat,' " says Hinkle. "He just laughed. He said, 'No, Tony, five thousand would just make things worse. If you can figure out how to squeeze in another hundred thousand, let me know.' "

By the '40s Indiana smoldered with basketball "hotbeds," clusters of settlements where three generations of rivalry had made basketball the strongest thread in the

52

community fabric. The meeting of cowhide and maple had become the Hoosier drumbeat.

Dubois County, an unlikely pocket of German and Dutch settlements, was as hot as a hotbed got. The towns have names like Holland, Jasper, Huntingburg, Schnellville, Bretzville and St. Marks. Many residents are connected by a common Bavarian heritage, but there are, mind you, distinctions, especially at sectional time: the good burghers of Jasper were said to speak "Low Dutch," while folks from Ferdinand, eight miles away, spoke "High Dutch."

Likewise, Jasper was Catholic, Huntingburg Protestant. After a contest between the two, the winners grew to expect a call from the losers in the middle of the night. A voice would scream "Catlicker!" or "Potlicker!"—whichever the occasion demanded—into the phone, and then it would go dead.

It could get nasty. When Holland upset Huntingburg in the 1952 sectional, the citizens of Huntingburg nearly starved Holland out by canceling deliveries of milk from the Holland dairy. In the '60s, when the Holland and Huntingburg schools consolidated—a move violently opposed by Holland, which lost its high school—the lone Holland school board member who voted in favor of the merger found his barn in flames one evening.

In 1951 Huntingburg went for the groin. In a successful attempt to seize what had been the Jasper sectional, they built a gym that could have held everyone in the county, that is, everyone except for Jasperites. Not a bad idea, come to think of it. Still, each year at sectional time they had to build temporary seats to hold the overflow crowds. This led to perhaps uniquely Hoosier liability problems.

One year, an elderly man reached down to find his seat in the temporary bleachers and got his finger stuck between

Barnstorming Indianapolis *News* reporter William Fox and Butler University coach Tony Hinkle prepare to board a Stutz Bearcat for their annual tour of the sixteen final schools in the tourney. During the last years of this event, they found themselves racing an airplane. *(Courtesy Herb Schwomeyer, Hoosier Hysteria and Hersteria, Inc.)*

Fifty thousand of Hammond's 70,000 residents greet Hammond Technical High's 1940 state champions at ten o'clock on a Sunday morning. *(Indianapolis News)* (RIGHT)

A massive parade through downtown Fort Wayne celebrates South Side High's 1938 state championship. *(Nieman
Studio)*

Arthur Trester, feared and respected architect of the Indiana high school tourney, at his show palace, 15,000-seat Butler Field House. *(Courtesy Dale Glenn)*

Fairmount High's clutch-shooting guard James Dean, later the "Rebel Without a Cause." *(Fairmount Historical Museum)* (LEFT)

Eighteen of America's 20 biggest high school gyms are in Indiana; 150 facilities seat over 3,000. In 1951, the year of this photo, the Huntingburg gym could hold twice the town's population and 20 times the student enrollment. *(Chase Studio)*

a board and a crossbrace. When his row sat down after the National Anthem, his fingertip was severed. "He came into school the next day looking for his fingertip," says Dale Glenn, the Huntingburg coach at the time. "His wife told him to go find it, but he didn't want to miss the game. He was hoping we'd kept it for him."

The ticketless would do anything to get inside. Once, two guys walked past the ticket window, each with a fifty-pound block of ice slung over his back between wooden tongs. "Concessions," they mumbled, heads down, ballcaps pulled down low. Once past, they ditched the ice—and the tongs—in the restroom and headed upstairs. The halftime mob had to wade to the urinals.

The seat of Dubois County is Jasper, a town from the Rhine that somehow turned up in Hoosierland. Nearly all the restaurants feature sausage and *Bier*. The streets are lined with prim red-brick houses which stand in contrast to the white frame dwellings in surrounding towns. The Jasper phone book is a marvel of vowel postponement, especially at the S's.

"While I was growin' up, Jasper was 95 percent German, Catholic and Democratic, and 100 percent white," says sportswriter Jerry Birge, 47. "I remember the Greyhound'd stop at Wilson's Drug Store, and now and then my buddies'd come runnin' back to me sayin', 'Hurry, there's one in there eatin'.' All us kids'd climb up to the window to watch a black guy eat. That'd be a big event."

Birge was in fifth grade the year of the Miracle. The night before he was to go back from Christmas vacation to St. Joseph's grade school, run by the Providence nuns, the Wildcat whistle woke his family. Sirens sounded everywhere. In nightclothes, his family scrambled to the crest of a hill and watched the grade school burn to the ground. Three days later, the nuns had arranged for the kids to share Jasper High School, the teenagers attending in the morning and the children in the afternoon.

"Come February, when the sectional started, it was really exciting for us little kids to see all the halls decorated, and all the signs sayin' "Good luck, Wildcats," says Birge. "But we were almost laughing about Jasper's chances to win the sectional. Winslow was undefeated. Huntingburg was ranked. Holland had a great team.

"Well, this one nun, Sister Joan, stood up in class and said, 'Kids, don't worry, I've got it all figured out.' She was a real sports nut, had all sorts of Notre Dame stuff on her desk. She said, 'Jasper's going to win the state championship this year.' We thought she'd finally lost it. She said, 'Look on the calendar. The state finals are going to be on St. Joseph's feast day.' She was right, March 19. We said, 'So what?' 'Well,' she said, 'we're from St. Joseph's school, and God's going to reward Jasper High for lettin' us use their school.' "

No one could have blamed Birge and his pals for laughing. Jasper High School had finished the 1949 regular season 11–9, fourth in their local conference. They had lost four of their last five games. It would dignify their status to say they were unranked.

The Wildcats were coached by Leo C. ("Cabby") O'Neill, a former baseball and basketball star at the University of Alabama. Cabby had the courtside manner of a drill sergeant. He believed that basketball boiled down to fundamentals: If you learn it right in practice, you'll do it right in the games.

The Jasper squad had its share of rough kids. Some of

them had a hard time taking O'Neill's regimen. One who could take anything Cabby could dish out and seemed to want even more was a little kid named Bobby White. White was a good little shooter with a nice head for the game, but he'd stopped growing at 5'6" and 135 pounds. Cabby cut him from the team as a freshman and sophomore, but the kid kept hanging around the gym after school, pestering Cabby for at least a chance to scrimmage with the teams.

Cabby gave in and kept him but rarely used him as a junior and had no special plans for him as a senior until after the first game of the season. It was then that someone reported to Cabby that one of his regulars had been seen smoking a cigarette. Cabby summoned the boy, wrung a confession out of him and stripped him of his uniform.

The next game, when Bobby White was announced in the starting lineup, the gym thundered with boos. It was a pointed finger. Everyone was sure White had ratted on the dismissed player. They couldn't prove it, and he denied it again and again, but that didn't matter. Evidence was not a factor. To them, it was just *like* Bobby White.

White was, in the vernacular of the day, a "clean Gene," one who didn't hang out, an outsider who had moved into Japser too late to have grown up on the grade school teams with the other kids. He kept his nose in his schoolbooks, and, worst of all, the nuns seemed to love him.

They knew he went to Mass every day, but until later they didn't know what he was talking to God about. Every morning for years he'd prayed he could that day improve himself so he could help Jasper win the state championship when he was a senior.

His life was focused like a laser. "I'd go to Mass, go to school and go to practice," White recalls. "Then I'd get off from practice about 4:00, get a sandwich and go back and play until about 9:00." For ten years the prayer was the same. "The concept was to *win* the state championship," he says. "I prayed to improve myself so I could contribute more."

"I was in a play with his mother, Louise, once," says Jerry Birge, "and we got to talking about Bobby. She said she told him, 'Son, if it doesn't happen, please don't lose faith. She said he told her, 'Don't worry, Mom. We'll win.'"

Two headlines juxtaposed in a mid-February Jasper *Daily Herald* convey Jasper's priorities as the tourney approached:

"Winslow Draws Tournament Bye"
"Munich Spy Trials Partially Opened"

The Wildcats somehow beat Dubois, Holland and Huntingburg in the sectional. When they fell behind the Winslow Eskimos 24–14 at halftime of the final game, Jasper fans were thinking that at least they'd have bragging rights all summer long. Again, there were things they didn't know.

"I remember Cabby O'Neill walking up the ramp to start the second half and saying to me, 'I want you to take it over and make it happen,'" recalls Bobby White. As the next morning's *Daily Herald* put it, Jasper roared from behind to beat Winslow 48–39 "on the sensational, hard driving of little Bobby White." Quietly, after the sectional win, the other Catholic boys on the squad began to go to Mass with Bobby.

Tourney fever had consumed Jasper. The next Saturday's headlines tell the story:

"Battle Today for Regional Title"
"Employee of Justice Dept., Russ. Diplomat, Seized"

They nipped Monroe City 57–55 for the regional title, again coming from behind. The Jasper *Daily Herald* reported that "the first three rows [of Jasper fans] went repeatedly onto the floor to protest calls." The following morning, Bobby White noticed a throng at Mass, including some Protestant teammates.

The next week, forward Bill Litchfield, a poor shooter, banged one home at the buzzer to beat Bloomington for the semistate title. Most of the town dragged themselves out of bed and went to Mass that morning. Something unusual was definitely happening here.

Jasper's local radio station, WITZ, had broadcast the Wildcat games all year long, but the huge forty-eight-station network out of Indianapolis had the license for the tourney. It was damned insulting to hear the slickers make fun of the German names. *Schutz schoots!* was only so funny after the hundredth time.

The WITZ engineers decided to do something about it. License or no license, the Wildcats were in the finals, and God knew when they'd get there again. Very illegally, they pirated a frequency assigned to a Canadian clear-channel station that had already signed off, summoned the local announcers, and put WITZ back on the air over a four-mile radius.

The Friday before the state finals, the *Daily Herald* featured ads like the following:

"NOTICE:
Our office will be closed Saturday, March 19,
to give our employees a chance

to boost the Wildcats to victory.
—Link Twins Loan Co. (Over Flick's Drug Store)"

On March 19 Jasper roared from behind twice to win the championship, the final game a 62–61 thriller against Madison. The Jasper-Madison final is still remembered as one of the best games ever played in Indiana. The lead changed constantly; the pressure was crushing. In the final minute, Cabby O'Neill glanced over at his rival coach, Ray Eddy, and found Eddy looking back at him. In the heat of it all, each had seemed to realize how special that moment was, that maybe there would never be another like it, and had turned to catch sight of the only other person who could know in the same way. Cabby winked, and Eddy winked back.

It was the damnedest thing. Jasper had won the tourney by rallying from behind in eight consecutive tourney games. A few smaller schools had won the tourney, but no champion had ever started out with less momentum.

How did they do it? It seemed like everyone in Jasper had a hand in it. Maybe it was because Mrs. Dr. St. John Lukemeyer had kept her vow never to stop pacing during the tourney until Jasper had won. Maybe it was Bill Litchfield's dad's hat, which never came off until the final buzzer against Madison. Maybe those who found magic in the three consecutive nine-point sectional victory margins had it right. And of course, the tourney was won on St. Joseph's feast day.

Bobby White, who seemed to contribute more with each game, scored twenty points in the final contest. His prayers had been answered. Of course there had been no reason for his mother to worry. A few days later, the nuns of the local order gave Bobby a plaque bearing Rudyard Kipling's poem "If" in recognition of his influence on the religious life of the community.

For his part, Cabby O'Neill, now 79 and still active in Jasper affairs, professes little expertise about miracles. He is a basketball coach. "I know more people came to church when we started winnin'," says Cabby, "but I wasn't at the door countin' heads. That wasn't my line of work."

"Let Joy Be Unconfined," blared the *Daily Herald*, "for we have crashed the circle of the basketball elite. This morning, the former Jasperites who are living in almost any part of the U.S. can point proudly to the sports pages or the front pages and say to anybody within earshot, 'Brother, that's my hometown, good old Jasper.' "

Hoosier basketball chauvinism reached a peak of sorts during World War II, which gave Hoosiers a grand occasion to spread the gospel to other GIs. To hear some of them tell it, the best players reported to the gym, suffered floor-burns and spent noncombat time teaching non-Hoosiers how to play.

"In 1944, when I was in the Navy," says Bob Collins, sports editor of the Indianapolis *Star*, settling back for a classic in the genre, "we had a barracks basketball team. Most of the guys were from Ohio and Minnesota. They were big, rawboned kids, and they played that same high-post game, a couple of fakes and the center shot." Collins illustrates this style expertly with leaden gestures.

"We played about three games and just got larruped. I went back to the barracks and said, 'I want to talk to everyone here from Indiana.' Some guys came up, and I said, 'Did you play? Did you play? Did you play?' Some had played in high school, some just in the schoolyard.

"I said, 'All right, we're going to be a team and we're going to play a game. We got one rule. The ball does *not* touch the floor.' We went out and beat those guys something like 75–30. We gave 'em Indiana basketball. When it was over, I said to those other guys, 'Now you know what basketball's about.'"

There was good reason for pride. To America's colleges, Indiana was "the basketball state," where the flatlands brought forth an annual cash crop of playmakers and rebounders. Scouts came in from everywhere at harvest time.

One year in the early '40s, all of Michigan State's starters were Hoosiers. In 1938, seven of the ten University of Southern California Trojans came from Indiana. When USC invaded the University of California that season, the Berkeley band struck up "Back Home Again in Indiana." Bobby White, who after Jasper played for Vanderbilt College, remembers a game against Ol' Miss in which twelve of the twenty players came from within a fifty-mile radius in southern Indiana. "It was like a homecoming," says White.

For a while it didn't hurt so badly because the emigrants cast glory on the homeland. Besides, some of their own were doing the harvesting. Nine coaches of Indiana high school champions had moved straight into head coaching jobs for major colleges. Everett Case, who spent much of the '20s and '30s in Arthur Trester's doghouse for recruiting high school kids away from their hometowns, later established and popularized college basketball in Dixie by filling his North Carolina State lineups with Hoosier kids.

But in 1948 it went a little too far. That year, while Indiana University finished in the Big Ten cellar, Kansas University stole away 6'9" Clyde Lovellette, the state's best college prospect. Case took several others. After the University of Kentucky won the 1948 NCAA championship, their hated coach rubbed it in. "Indiana has not only lost its leadership as the top basketball state," gloated Adolph Rupp, "but the South has replaced the Midwest as the home of basketball."

Indiana University coach Branch McCracken declared war. He announced that henceforth he would recruit only five boys a year, the five best Indiana players. He asked the state's high school coaches—his lieutenants in this crusade—to identify and bring forward these special young men. To ease the transition, he taught coaches the "McCracken system," a pell-mell fast break style ridiculed in the East as "firehouse basketball." Wherever they went, the best seniors heard people tell them, "You're too good to play anywhere but Indiana." And in 1953 Indiana won the NCAA championship with ten Hoosier small-town boys.

It seemed like a wonderful dance, one that had gone on for three generations and would go on forever. Until eternity, little towns would mill out thick-waisted sharpshooters who would walk out of fields and from under hoods and into college lineups. No matter how many wars and depressions, at least Indiana would always produce the most and best basketball players: Indiana would always be a small town, and it would always be Friday night.

But seeds of change were already in the wind. In 1940, Hammond Tech won the tourney. It was a big-city school from the Calumet region, a place that always seemed to belong to Chicago. Hammond's players had strange-sounding surnames: Bicanic, Shimala, Kielbowicz and Abatie. Like Lebanon or Martinsville, Hammond had a victory parade, but its drew a crowd of 50,000 on a Sunday morning.

In 1951 the world shrank again. WFBM in Indianapolis began to televise the tournament. The next year WTTV began its immortal telecasts of the Indiana University games, which began with announcer Paul Lennon holding up a bag of Chesty Potato Chips and stating, "I've got my ticket; have you got yours?" Suddenly kids in Bloomington and Indianapolis could see the images of players from Wisconsin and Ohio without leaving their homes.

By the early '50s, black players were no longer isolated figures in small-town team photos but were instead four and five—and often the best—players on city teams. Indianapolis Crispus Attucks High, one of three all-black schools which had been banned from the tourney until 1942, made the final four in 1951. Their players seemed to play a different game, somewhere up in the air.

A kid named Jim Dean, a nice little guard from Fairmont High who in 1949 had beaten Gas City with a last-ditch shot in the Marion sectional, was now James Dean, a big-time movie star who seemed to be getting famous by sneering back at everything that had made him. *Rebel Without a Cause* summed it up pretty nicely.

In 1954 Wingate High School—Stoney's school—simply disappeared. In an effort to bring better facilities to rural schoolchildren, Wingate had been merged with five other little country schools to form something called "North Montgomery."

For a half-century's winters the excitement had crackled on Friday night. Really, going to the games had been a lot like going to church. You came together in a room built wide and high enough for the spirit to swoop and soar. Each had its iconography, the saints or apostles in one room and the team photos in another. Winter after winter, the prospect of vengeance had brought the community together on

Friday night and the hope of redemption had reconvened it at daybreak on Sunday.

In March 1954 the curtain came down on the farm boy era that had begun when Reverend Nicholas McKay had crossed the Ohio line with a way to improve the peach basket. After the 1954 tourney, fourteen of the next seventeen champions came from big-city schools. But the final act was to be the most remembered sporting event in Indiana history. It was high drama worthy of everything that had gone on before.

MILAN

HIGH SCHOOL:

The

Hoosier Dream

The telephone shatters Bobby Plump's deep sleep. His fingers encounter the receiver on the third ring. Plump drags it across the pillow to his ear. There is music. Laughter. He glances at the clock: 2:15 A.M. "Hello, man . . . is this Bobby Plump?" The caller's voice is thick. This is not an insurance call. It's the other call, the one he hears almost as much.

"Yes, it is."

"Are you the one that hit the shot?"

"Yeah."

"Well, we was bettin' here whether the score was 31–30 or 32–30 when you hit that shot. Can you help us out?"

Many Hoosier kids discover their roots at the Indiana Basketball Hall of Fame, a blocky limestone shrine in downtown Indianapolis. Each year busloads of schoolkids from Muncie and Anderson, Plymouth, Gary, Fort Wayne and South Bend race around the rooms full of trophy cases and yellowed headlines. They laugh at basketballs stretched and laced like corsets over inflated bladders, gawk at primitive shoes that once held calloused feet—and in which only a god could have dunked—and argue about which championship game film the group ought to watch.

They pause to admire Oscar Robertson's photograph ("Dad

says pound for pound he was the best player that ever was."
"Musta weighed a lot less than Bird, then."). They try to
tell the Van Arsdale twins apart and rave about Steve Alford, the latest megahero.

At some point, at least one kid usually stumbles into a
room that is different from all the others. "Hey, what's this
. . . there ain't nothin' in here but a TV set." The children
are drawn deeper into the carpeted sanctum, which indeed
contains nothing but a huge mahogany console with a small
screen near the top. Below the screen are strips of red
plastic tape that bear the words: "1954 State Final: Muncie
vs. Milan. Bobby Plump's Famous Game Winning Shot.
Press Button to Start."

Captured in those few seconds of scratchy, silent film
is the Hoosier dream. It is there to remind all Hoosiers
that old-fashioned values—hard work, boldness and imagination—will still prevail in a fair fight. And if the world
no longer seems a fair fight, the tourney comes around each
March to remind everyone what it used to be like before
the deck was stacked.

All other states but Delaware and Kentucky have divided
their state basketball tourney into classes by enrollment.
Typically, big-city schools play in one tourney, medium-
sized and rural schools in events of their own. In Indiana,
little country schoolhouses confront great city institutions
named Washington and Central and Lincoln in the same
tournament. Not as many kids get trophies in Indiana, but,
if you can win, you wake up not as the champ of Division
II-A but as the ruler of all Hoosierland.

But only once have Hoosiers had a chance to savor the
upset the event was designed to produce. That was in 1954,

73

when Milan High School, with an enrollment of 161 students—seventy-three boys—brought down Muncie Central High School, a school ten times as big, to win a tournament in which 751 schools were entered. The game was won on a shot with three seconds left by a kid named Bobby Plump.

It has been estimated that on that day in March, 90 percent of all Indiana families were watching or listening to the game. Along with the events of World War II and the births, deaths and passages of loved ones, it is one of the most remembered events in the lives of many Hoosiers. Milan struck a blow for the small, the rural, the stubborn; Milan stopped the highway, saved the farm and allowed many to believe that change was just an option.

By hitting a fifteen-foot jump shot, Bobby Plump delivered the dream to which many grateful Hoosiers still cling. That is why Plump's sleep gets interrupted—more and more these days—and why one moment in his adolescence is enshrined in Indianapolis in a room all its own.

Bobby Plump grew up in Pierceville, Indiana, population 45, about thirty miles northwest of Cincinnati. He is the youngest of six children, raised by his father and eldest sister after his mother died when he was 5.

It was not an easy life, but the Plumps were not the kind to complain about what they didn't have. Bobby's father taught school for a while, but when the Depression hit he took on a chicken route to Cincinnati, selling eggs until he found factory work in Lawrenceburg.

There was a good roof over their heads, but nothing unnecessary under it. There was never running water, and no electricity until Bobby was 12. Four years later they were finally able to bring home a refrigerator, but phones and television sets were always to be for others. It was a warm and supportive family, and Plump today recalls his as a wonderful childhood.

"I may have run the world's smallest paper route," he says, "but I always had some money. I think I delivered eighteen or twenty papers. We had it for twenty-four years. When you got six kids, after the two brothers came back from the war, you could always get a card game up. We used to play pinochle with an Alladin lamp. Dad did the trading—that's what he called it—in town every Saturday. He'd go to the Oddfellows Hall, and if we had a dime we'd go to the movies, five cents to get in and five cents for popcorn. Then we'd meet him back over at one of the stores and ride back to Pierceville. It was a wonderful time."

"Town" was Milan, a center for Ripley County's hog, tobacco, poultry and cattle markets, whose population was about 1,100. Though it was named after the Italian city, it is pronounced *My*-lan. For the record, you can also find Athens, Cairo, Paris, Rome, Shanghai and Vienna in Indiana.

A town of 1,100 could seem a jungle to a Piercevillian. "I remember getting lost in Milan in fifth or sixth grade," recalls Plump. "I went to a movie and couldn't find anybody. I was standing there crying and a man working in a furniture factory saw me and picked me up and brought me home. I just didn't know my way around."

When Bobby was in fourth grade, his father nailed a backboard to a shed for him on Christmas Day. Bobby spent most of the day shooting at it, entranced. He soon could hit the basket regularly. Better still, before long he found that he could freeze whoever was guarding him with a fake and a quick stride to the basket.

In 1949 Plump heard his first Indiana high school basketball tournament on the radio. He and Glenn Butte, who lived across the tracks, made it a grand occasion. They strung up some lights out back and together they choreographed the play-by-play, imagining how the players looked and moved.

In the final game, Bobby was Madison's Dee Monroe and Glenn played Jasper's Bobby White. Thirty years later, when Plump was introduced to Bobby White at a hall of fame banquet, he was astonished to discover that White was only 5'6". Assuming he was much taller, they had choreographed the shots all wrong.

Even in a community of 45, it was easy to get ten or twelve players up after dinner, when everyone came home. You played with the older kids, your brothers, fathers and in-laws. The games were rough, especially on a gravel surface; "No blood, no foul" was the Pierceville court motto.

Bobby and Glenn and two other pals named Gene White and Roger Schroeder played together constantly. After a while, they developed a common experience of each other, each one understanding what the others were going to do on the court, the way voices in family quartets seem to reach for each other and blend.

Roger's family, the Schroeders, were the town merchants—they owned the one store in town—and day or night their place was the hub. At first everyone played in the barn behind the store, but the roof slanted down so you had to angle a shot from the corner too much. Besides, a nearby manure pile seemed to have a magnetic quality. So they moved the goal outside, trapped two shovels under a sheet of tin and strung electric lights between them; that way they could keep playing until midnight.

In the winters everyone went into Milan to see the big

high school play basketball. Milan's was not a glorious tradition. Over the decades the school had won two or three sectional tourneys but had never won a game in the regionals. Batesville, one of the other big schools in Ripley County along with Osgood and Versailles, beat Milan so regularly in the county tourney that it became a sort of custom, something you expected.

The Pierceville kids were especially attracted to a Milan player named Bill Gorman. Rather than lifting his leg mechanically and hoisting up one-handed push shots like everyone else or stopping to twirl the ball like a squirrel sizing up a nut and then lofting a two-hand set shot, Gorman leaped in the air on the run or off the dribble and fired up the first jump shots anyone around had seen. Gorman died in Korea in 1952, but he left his legacy in his jump shot.

From first grade on, they all went to school in Milan. That meant a three-mile walk or bike ride home, unless somebody's parents could find the time to go in and pick them up. They felt clumsy and ill-dressed around the Milan kids, who seemed to have a zest for ridiculing them.

Plump was painfully shy and easily embarrassed. He tells a story about two Milan kids tearing off his new green coat and throwing it in the snow. The memory still brings color to his cheeks and causes his voice to break. He became a legend at Milan, but he remains a Piercevillian at heart, and to him there remains a living difference between the two.

Four Piercevillians—Plump, Schroeder, Butte and White—made the eighth-grade team at Milan. Here at last was a way to shine. Milan, too, had skilled players who had grown up together. The team lost only one game all year and began to attract the attention of the town. In Milan's coffee shops it was said that these kids were "comers." The stigma of being from the country meant nothing in such quarters; hell, you could be from Mars and it'd be just fine if you could shoot.

Milan's varsity coach was Herman ("Snort") Grinsted, a veteran high school coach whose nickname derived from his explosive temper. Grinsted quickly recognized Plump's shooting ability and began to plan for the future. Though one-handed shots or even overhanded free-throws had been forbidden in grade school, Grinsted told Plump as a freshman to perfect one move: start with the ball on one side of the court or the other, dribble across to the free-throw line and then stop and shoot the one-handed jumper.

By the time Plump was a sophomore, he and two other classmates were dressing for the varsity games, but not really expecting to play much on a team with seven seniors. Then, early in the season, county rival Osgood humiliated Milan 85–38, and after the game Snort erupted. Red-faced, he banished all seven seniors from the team and moved three sophomores, including Plump, into the starting lineup.

No Ripley County team beat Milan again for the rest of the season, and twice they avenged their loss to Osgood. The team was the toast of Milan. Plump remembers being late for class one Monday after he had played especially well. He approached the classroom door, embarrassed as usual about his clothing, in mortal terror of standing out. He gathered himself outside the door and opened it. When he appeared, his classmates stood up and applauded. "It was then I really knew I had something going for me," he says.

Grinsted, on cloud nine, rewarded his young charges by buying everyone new uniforms at the end of the year. When the word got out, Milan's principal was furious. He summoned Grinsted and pointed out that the athletic fund was now broke and this time Snort had gone way too far. Shaken, Snort offered to pay for the uniforms himself, but it was too late. Like his seven exiled seniors, he was a man without a team.

There was a good reason for all the grumbling you could hear around Milan in the summer of 1953. Snort was gone. Some thanks, after the year he'd had. And to make matters worse, the guy they hired to replace him was twenty-four years old, two years out of college and, rumor was, he was a set-offense man.

Indiana at that time had achieved an identity as the heart of "racehorse" basketball. Most high school coaches took their cues from Branch McCracken's Indiana University squads—the "Hurryin' Hoosiers"—whose greyhounds usually won games by scores like 102–99. To slow the game down on purpose was worse than soft; in Ripley County it was damn near treasonous.

After Grinsted, Marvin Wood was indeed going to take some getting used to. He was a soft-spoken, highly disciplined and religious young man. In all the years Bobby Plump was to know Wood, he heard Wood raise his voice in anger only once, and on that occasion—after the team turned in a sloppy performance in a tournament game— Wood kicked a medicine chest and injured his foot.

Wood was convinced that these smart, sharpshooting kids could win by using the offensive system he'd learned from Tony Hinkle, his coach at Butler University. He knew firsthand that its inherent order could neutralize faster and taller players. Hinkle's system amounted to fourteen variations of a simple pattern involving two players. The trick was to execute the plays perfectly. On your first day at Butler you began to learn the fourteen patterns. On your last day you were teaching them to the plebes.

Wood had been all set to sign a contract to coach at Bloomfield High when his high school coach told him of the sudden opening at Milan and advised Wood to go down and check it out. Word was, there was some real talent down there.

So one summer morning Wood drove to Ripley County, sat down on a basketball and watched two groups of youngsters, one in Milan and one in Pierceville, play game after game. They were small but quick, smart and good shooters. Above all, they were obviously close friends, kids who acted like they had been born playing together. Though the money—$4,000 to teach and coach—wasn't as good as the Bloomfield job, Wood applied for and won the job at Milan.

Wood's first challenge of the 1953 season was a personnel matter: fifty-eight of Milan's seventy-three boys tried out for the team. And, as much as Wood disliked zone defenses, that was the only way they had ever played. At first Wood tried to force them to play man-to-man, but he soon gave up and asked the junior high coach to show him how they had learned to play defense.

Wood imposed few rules, but he enforced them relentlessly. He set a 10:00 curfew during the regular season, but on New Year's Eve he let the players stay out till 1:00 A.M. On that evening Bobby Plump and a teammate were double-dating. A flat tire stalled them, but the quartet managed to pull up to Plump's house at the stroke of one, at least according to Plump's watch. Wood was waiting for them; his watch said they had just missed. There was no debate. As Plump recalls it, Wood said quietly, "I'm going to make an example of you." Plump did not dress for the next game.

The next-to-the-last game of the regular season, Milan was drubbing Osgood again when things started getting rough. Wood called a time-out. Explaining that he didn't want anyone getting hurt before the sectional started, he told the team to try something totally new.

He stationed Plump in the middle of the court, put Ray Craft and Bob Engels deep in the corners near midcourt and told Gene White and Ron Truitt to stand in the corners down under the basket. He instructed Plump simply to hold the ball until someone tried to take it away from him. When that happens, he said, someone come out and meet the ball so Bobby can get rid of it and everybody else cut toward the basket and look for a pass. When the players asked him about it later, it turned out Wood even had a name for the scheme—he called it the "Cat and Mouse." Hoosiers proudly claim it as the forerunner of all spread offenses today.

Entering the tourney, everyone in Ripley County knew Milan had a fine team. They'd had to move their last few home games to a bigger gym, and, for the first time in a long while, the school had had to raffle sectional tickets to meet the demand. Chris Volz, Milan's GM dealer, stood up at a rally and promised the team a fleet of Chevies to drive to the sectionals. There was a lusty cheer. Hold it, Volz said, that's not all. It's gonna be Pontiacs for the regionals, Buicks for the semistate and Cadillacs for the finals. The Caddies must have felt secure in their showroom: Milan had never won even a regional game.

Milan breezed through the sectionals and headed off in Pontiacs to the Rushville regional tourney. There they got lucky. In a cliffhanger against Morton Memorial, Milan fell behind by two points with twenty-eight seconds left. The ball went out of bounds, and while it was being retrieved the timekeeper forgot to turn the clock off. When play resumed, Milan's Bill Jordan was quickly fouled, and when he looked at the clock, he was amazed to see that there was no time left. Calmly he hit both free throws and tied the game. Morton appealed without success. Plump won the game for Milan with two free throws in a second overtime.

Milan went all the way to Indianapolis before losing to South Bend Central in the afternoon semifinal game. Plump had a great tournament, scoring nineteen of Milan's thirty-seven points against Central. It had been an unbelievable season, highlighted by one of the most remarkable coaching jobs in Indiana high school history: a rookie coach had taken a school with seventy-three boys to the state finals. Snort Grinsted was all but forgotten, and Marvin Wood had every right to feel like a king. Instead, he was miserable.

All summer he blamed himself for having let his team down. They deserved more, he told himself. Maybe a more experienced coach could have given them the chance for which they had worked so hard. He thought about quitting.

At one point during his torment Wood was approached by a man who owned a tavern in Milan. He said he had a son, 6'4", who lived with his grandparents in Lawrenceburg and was a good ball player. He said he knew Milan's center was graduating and that Wood was going to be left with Gene White as a 5'11" pivotman. If Wood said the word, he'd board the boy in Milan next year. Marvin Wood declined politely, explaining that it wouldn't be fair to the kids who were already there.

Wood pulled himself together and took the reins again.

Milan's Bobby Plump fires away against South Bend
Central in the 1953 tourney. *(Courtesy Bob Plump)*

Milan's cheering section—most prominently Bobby
Plump's sister and brother-in-law—fourth quarter, 1954
state finals. *(Courtesy Bob Plump)*

The day Hoosierland stood still: Bobby Plump holds the
ball for over four minutes as Muncie Central's Jimmy
Barnes stands ready. *(Courtesy Bob Plump)* (LEFT)

Glen Butte, Roger Schroeder, Bobby Plump and Gene White, mid-town Pierceville. *(Courtesy Bob Plump)* (LEFT)

Hoosier immortals, the 1954 Milan Indians: front row, left to right: Bob Engel, Ron Truitt, Gene White, Bobby Plump, Ray Craft. Between front and back rows: Roger Schroeder. Back row: Glen Butte, Ken Wendelman, Rollin Cutter, Bill Jordan, Assistant Coach Clarence Kelley, Motorcycle cop Pat Stark and Coach Marvin Wood. *(Indianapolis News)*

The 1954 group bolted off along the same path as their predecessors, losing only twice during the regular season. Seven hundred fifty-one schools entered the tourney that year, and again few took Milan seriously. A schedule that included Rising Sun, Napoleon, Aurora and Montezuma simply did not excite the Indianapolis sportswriters, whose hearts were hardened against the favorite-son teams which dissolved annually before big crowds in exotic cities.

But this team was for real. Milan rolled through the sectional and regional rounds of the tournament, flattening its first five opponents by an average of nineteen points. In Chris Volz's big Buicks, they cruised into Indianapolis for the semistate tourney with something to prove.

They beat Montezuma 44–34 in the afternoon semifinal, then went back to the Pennsylvania Hotel for a nap before the night game against Indianapolis Crispus Attucks, an all-black high school. "When we went out to dinner that night," recalls Plump, "an unusual number of people followed us around. One of the frequent remarks we heard was, 'C'mon Milan, beat those niggers.' People were saying it every-where."

Crispus Attucks was led by the great Oscar Robertson, who in 1954 was a 6'3" sophomore forward. Attucks was a strong, savvy and spectacular team, a year away from in-vincibility. Milan raced to a strong first-half lead, but the effort exhausted Plump. At halftime he was seized by cramps in both legs and broke into a cold sweat. Wood wrapped him in a blanket and told him to stay in the locker room, the others would hold the lead. When Wood walked up-stairs for the second half, Plump was already out on the floor warming up. His twenty-eight points led Milan to a 65–52 victory.

The next weekend, when the team fired up the Caddies

for the state finals in Indianapolis, 900 of the town's 1,100 residents went with them. Milan swamped a fine Terre Haute Gerstmeyer team in the afternoon game but still entered the evening showcase against Muncie Central as definite underdogs.

Muncie Central was—and still is—a big school with an intimidating tradition. The Bearcats had won the state championship four times, more than any other school. Muncie played its home games in a gym that could hold seven times the entire population of Milan. But the pressing problem was that Muncie's front line averaged 6'4"; by contrast, Milan's Gene White jumped center at 5'11".

Wood thought carefully about the job ahead. Nervousness would not be a problem. These kids had played together since they'd worn braces, and they weren't the kind to scare anyway. And nobody had taken them seriously enough for the fear of failure to enter in. But there was just no way a conventional approach could offset Muncie's height and muscle. Wood decided, for the first time, to try the spread offense, the Cat and Mouse, for a whole game.

The strategy worked like a charm for the first half, and Milan took a 25–17 lead into the locker room. Now all they had to do was stay calm and hit the shots that surely would come once Muncie started to press. But the third quarter was catastrophic: Milan failed to hit a single field goal and entered the final eight minutes of the game tied 26–26.

Most Hoosiers over 40 can tell you where they were during the final period of that game. Statewide television coverage of the finals had begun only three years before, but there had been a sophisticated radio network since 1921, and of course Butler Field House was jammed with over 15,000 Hoosiers. The state stood still that Saturday night, and the dream shimmered.

Muncie pulled ahead by two points in the opening seconds. Gambling that his veteran team would prevail in the frenzy that was sure to come, Wood stuck to his game plan. He told Plump, just as if they were playing Osgood for bragging rights to Ripley County, to stand there and hold the ball until someone came out to get it.

So for four minutes and thirteen seconds Plump stood with the ball cradled under one arm, the other hand on his hip, staring at Jimmy Barnes, the player assigned to guard him. Barnes stared back, knees flexed, arms extended in a defensive position.

Most of Indiana thought Wood was insane, and many Hoosiers were furious. As the clock wound down, it sounded for all the world on the radio like Milan was *quitting*; Wood seemed to be mocking everything that every father told every son. They were *behind*, for Christ's sake, and they weren't even *trying* and the dream was ticking away.

Plump recalls those moments: "I kept looking over at the bench and Marvin Wood was sitting there as if he was out on the porch. He had his legs crossed, kicking his foot. If he would have told me to throw the ball up in the stands I would have done it, I had that much confidence in him. But when I'd look at him he'd just put his hands up, like 'Everything's okay.'"

Jimmy Barnes was likewise glancing over at Muncie coach Jay McCreary, who, ahead, was quite content to let time expire. "We wanted to go out and guard 'em, but coach said to lay back," recalls Barnes. "I wanted him to put the ball on the floor, 'cause I figured I could steal it from anyone."

With about two minutes left, the frenzy began: Wood let Plump shoot for the tie. He missed, and Muncie got the rebound, but then Milan's zone press forced a turnover

90

and Ray Craft tied it at 28-all. Muncie coughed the ball up again, and Plump put Milan ahead with two free throws. Muncie's Gene Flowers retied the score at 30. With all of Hoosierland on its feet, ear to the radio, eyes on the tube or in the berserk field house itself, Plump and Craft brought the ball downcourt very slowly for the last time.

With eighteen seconds left, Wood called time out. In the huddle, Gene White suggested that everyone move to one side of the court and let Plump go one-on-one against Barnes. Plump was a little surprised since he was having a terrible game, having made only two of ten attempts so far. Wood agreed. Plump was the shooter and it was time for a shot.

Ray Craft was supposed to inbound the ball to Plump, and then the entire Milan team was to shift to the left side of the court, out of Plump's way. But Plump, who had felt jittery in the huddle, nearly blew the play right away. He took the ball out of bounds himself and threw it in to Craft, who somehow found the presence of mind to catch it and toss it back.

Then the nervousness disappeared. After all, it was the play Snort Grinsted had told him to perfect years before, and he had done it a million times out back and at Schroeder's and against Osgood and Cross Plains and Aurora.

Alone and with nothing to do but what he knew how to do better than anything in the world, Plump slowly worked the clock down to five seconds. Then he suddenly cut across the lane, stopped quickly at the top of the key, leaped in the air and flung the ball over Barnes's fingers and toward the hoop. As the ball sailed through, Goliath buckled, Excalibur slipped free from the rock and Indiana's dream came true.

* * *

When it was over, the 200 folks left in Milan rushed out to start a bonfire. It is fortunate that the blaze did not burn out of control, since twenty-one of Milan's twenty-four firemen were at the game.

To keep his team from being crushed by celebrants, Wood permitted a brief Cadillac parade, backwards, as it turned out, around the Indianapolis War Memorial Monument and then sequestered the boys in the Hotel Pennsylvania while joyous fans maintained a vigil outside.

They fired up the big Caddies for the last time and headed for Milan after breakfast on a bright Sunday morning. The caravan was led by Pat Stark, an Indianapolis motorcycle cop assigned to the team. They were expecting a celebration in town, maybe a brief homecoming in the Square, and then some sleep at last.

They were tickled to see the curbside crowds in the Indianapolis suburbs and thrilled by the fire trucks from Greensburg and Shelbyville that fell behind them on two-lane Highway 101. There were flags in all the little towns. Planes circled overhead. Officer Stark could not believe what was forming behind him, or ahead, for that matter.

About thirteen miles out of Milan, at Penntown, the team began to notice cars parked along the two-lane highway and met the first hikers waving and cheering and carrying picnic baskets. The motorcade had become a convoy, and they were losing speed. It took thirty-five minutes to go the eight miles from Batesville to Sunman. This was unreal.

When Officer Stark, flanked by American Legion cars, nosed into Milan, there were 40,000 people waiting. He turned off the Caddie and they all climbed onto a makeshift stage across from the park. From the stage, looking straight ahead, there were people as far as the eye could see. Kids dangled from the boughs of the sycamores in the park.

Everyone got to speak, even Stark. The big-city cop dissolved into tears. Marvin Wood repeated the four characteristics of a champion, the ones he had listed before every Milan game. They were: determination to win, self-confidence, alertness and luck. Mary Lou Wood, Marvin's wife, concluded her brief remarks with a line Bobby Plump was to use in the many speeches he would give after that day: "It's nice to be important," she said, "but it's more important to be nice."

"Plump" was the headline in the Indianapolis *Star* the following morning, and indeed Plump became a household word in Indiana. In fact, he remembers receiving a letter shortly after the tourney addressed "Plump, Indiana."

But it was still hard to get a totally swelled head in Pierceville. When the Indianapolis *Star* tried to telephone Plump to inform him that he was the new "Mr. Basketball"—the best player in the state—he still had to take the call at Schroeder's store. The phone went dead. He didn't find out for sure what they wanted until the next day.

Today Bobby Plump has his own insurance agency, one which provides nicely for his family. His first clients were college athletes, kids who were thrilled to meet him. He had impressive careers at Butler University—which he chose largely because he knew Tony Hinkle's fourteen two-man variations by heart, and he knew there would be lots of shots in it for him—and in amateur basketball, with the Phillips '66 Oilers. He very nearly made the 1960 Olympic team.

Hundreds of speeches and banquets and celebrity golf

93

tournaments have forced Bobby Plump—it's Bob now—to conquer his fear of public speaking; he says if he can get an early laugh he actually enjoys these appearances. He says that celebrity has taught him that everyone, even corporation presidents, has the basic insecurities. Though he still seems to have more fun talking about the pressure shots he missed than the one he made, he knows that he is forever consigned, like Don Larsen or Bobby Thompson, to recount his immortal jumper.

As the incarnation of the Dream, he is careful to tell an interviewer the whole story, with nothing left out, and as colorfully as possible. From time to time he'll say, "Wait, there's another story about that," or, "I forgot to tell you this," as if an omission would be irresponsible. Especially when you get to those final seconds, the stories peel away like layers from an onion. But the core is surprising: he says he really can't remember what he was thinking or what it felt like to hold the ball and look at Jimmy Barnes, except to recall, "He certainly was intense."

Jimmy Barnes is today a parole agent for the California State Prison System. He played college basketball for a year and was invited to an unsuccessful tryout with a professional team in 1961. Barnes says that although his relatives kid him a little about Milan when he goes back to Indiana, the people of Muncie did not hold Plump's shot against him. "They blamed everyone else but me, for some reason," he says. He and Plump, locked together in film and lore and a famous still photograph, have not met since they walked off the court that evening.

Each year the Milan teammates get together at Thanksgiving to retell the old stories. Milan's victory did more than provide memories for these players; nine out of ten received college scholarships, and eight graduated. Before that game almost no one from Milan had ever been able to afford college. "I asked my father one time," says Plump, "if I had not gotten a scholarship, would he have sent me to college. He said, 'No, I couldn't afford to send the other five. It would not have been right to borrow money to send you.'"

Plump is amazed by his enduring celebrity. Many Hoosier kids can tell you who Bobby Plump is, who he played for and that he hit a shot that won the tourney. But the years and the retellings have gnarled the events and lengthened the shot to a midcourt heave at the buzzer, often against their school.

Hardly a day goes by when someone doesn't mention the shot. "When I go to the bank to write a check, the people say, 'Hmmm, Plump, Milan—beat Muncie, hit the shot.'" His wife, Jenine, has learned to live with the calls in the middle of the night, and their three children, now grown, have had their own experiences with their father's legend:

"I was waitressing at this restaurant in 1981," recalls Tari Plump, Bob and Jenine's eldest daughter. "We were at a bar having drinks after work one night, and I still had my name tag on my blouse. There were two gentlemen sitting next to me with very pronounced foreign accents. One of them looked at my name tag and said, 'Tari Plump? Are you any relation to Bobby Plump?' I said, 'Yes, he's my father.' He got very excited. He said, 'I come to United States, arrive in New York, fly to Indianapolis. We talk about sports. All I hear is Bobby Plump, Bobby Plump . . . did he do something special?'"

4

THE
BLACK AND WHITE
OF
HOOSIER HYSTERIA:
Indianapolis
Crispus Attucks
High School

"The stone which the builders rejected is become the head of the corner."

—(MATTHEW 21:42)

This is how the Indianapolis *Recorder*, serving black Indianapolis, began its editorial of March 19, 1955: "It is with a spirit of profound reverence and thanksgiving that we hail the new high school basketball champions of Indiana, the Crispus Attucks Tigers. Persons unfamiliar with our State may believe that we are overdoing it in going down on our knees and giving praise to almighty God that this glorious thing has come to pass."

What had come to pass was not the end of a war. It was not that a tornado had skipped over Indianapolis, or that a vaccine had been discovered, or that rain had finally come. What had happened was that a basketball team had won a basketball game.

But of course, it wasn't an ordinary game or an ordinary team, and those weren't ordinary times. This victory sent black Indianapolis down to its knees in prayer and up again in jubilation because, while it didn't erase the sting of thirty years' injustice and ridicule, at least it made sure that black players could no longer be disregarded. On that evening the guard changed, and everyone knew it.

More than any other story, the rise of Crispus Attucks High School shows the power of basketball as a social force in Indiana. The school was established to isolate blacks at an insane time when the Ku Klux Klan controlled Indiana politics. Its teams were banned from the tourney for fifteen years and were shunned by white schools for years afterwards. With no gym to play in and wearing hand-me-down uniforms, this team had won far more than a basketball game on the night before the editorial: it had won a distinctively Hoosier form of redemption.

Attucks had also succeeded in removing a huge, burning embarrassment from Indianapolis. In forty-four years, no team from the state's biggest city had ever won the tourney. For many whites, for the first time it didn't matter that every kid who went to Attucks was black. What mattered was that *Indianapolis* Crispus Attucks had won. And while celebrating "our" team, everyone's team, many whites and blacks mingled with each other, spoke to each other, slapped each other on the back for the first time.

And when the party was over, the sobering prospect that Crispus Attucks would forever dominate the Indianapolis sectional tourney probably did more to integrate the public schools of Indianapolis than all the policy changes and loophole-ridden plans had ever done.

The *Recorder* goes on to explain, as if there were someone in Indiana who didn't know: "Basketball—especially the high school variety—occupies a particularly lofty place in the Hoosier scheme of things. It is far more than a boys' sport—in fact, it is just about the most important thing there is."

Or, as Attucks' great star Oscar Robertson put it, "I don't

want to take anything away from anyone else. But nobody did what we did."

Farming had never been an easy way to make a living in Indiana, not even in the rich till of central Indiana. That is, not until World War I. Then, for a few blessed seasons, everything changed: "Food Will Win the War" became the slogan, and suddenly you couldn't yank corn and beans out of the ground fast enough to feed Europe. Money started rolling in, money there had never been before, money to buy flivvers and feathered hats and player pianos.

With new cars, cash to burn and time on their hands, rural Hoosiers were ready for some action. The evangelists who had presented heaven as a blessed refuge from life's misery saw the flock slipping away; mortality wasn't turning out to be that bad a deal.

In 1926, Hoosier writer Samuel W. Tait, Jr., described the Ku Klux Klan's appeal: "Here at last," Tait wrote, "was a political weapon calculated to satisfy all the fears and hatreds the evangelical hell-hounds had been instilling in the faithful for so long: fear of the power of Rome; hatred of the wickedness of the cities; fear of the Darwinian heresy; and hatred of the evil individualist who persisted in having a private stock (of liquor)."

The Klan spread throughout many states in the '20s, but it roots sank deepest in Hoosier soil. "Nearly 500,000 Hoosiers, in white robes and hoods, burned their fiery crosses almost nightly to strike fear in the hearts of their neighbors," wrote journalist Irving Liebowitz. Roughly one in three white Hoosier males slipped under the sheet.

Even more remarkably, for a few dismal years in the '20s, the Klan took over Indiana's Republican Party—the party of Lincoln—which in turn controlled Hoosier politics. For a while, the most powerful figure in Indiana was a fiery demagogue named David C. Stephenson.

In 1921 Stephenson was in his late 20s, selling coal securities out of an Evansville hotel and wondering what to do next, when the call came. The Klan's Imperial Wizard, a Dallas dentist, said he had heard good things about Stephenson, heard that he could organize. He was willing to take a chance on Stephenson, to make him Grand Dragon of Indiana, to see what he could do. Stephenson had dabbled in Socialist politics and had even run for Congress as a Democrat, hoping the veterans who took in the stories he made up about his escapades as a war hero could put him over. All that had failed. He had nothing to lose.

Stephenson didn't waste time. He hired professional salesmen to spearhead recruiting drives. White Hoosiers received membership applications in the mail, on stationery with sketches of Klansmen on horseback. Stephenson dreamed up solemn mumbo jumbo rituals and nearly wore out the letter K. Women were Kamilias. The house organ, called the *Kourier*, featured a Klan Kiddie Korner. Memberships, called "Klectokons," went for between ten and twenty-five dollars, depending on your circumstances. Stephenson pocketed four dollars. White robes and peaked hats moved at six dollars a set, of which Stephenson kept $4.25. Hoosiers lapped it up; Stephenson raked in more than two million dollars in eighteen months.

January 12, 1925, may have been the dreariest day in Indiana's history. On that day the Klan vote swept in a new governor, Ed Jackson, who, campaigning on the Republican ticket in Stephenson's Cadillac, had captured ninety of Indiana's ninety-two counties. The tide also brought dozens of legislators, prosecutors, judges and mayors.

Business executives filed into Stephenson's mansion in Indianapolis, cash in hand, shopping for help at the Statehouse. Intolerance had become fashionable. Hoosiers threw sheets over their heads and formed vigilante squads, terrorizing blacks, Jews and Catholics, tarring women accused of being prostitutes. There were public floggings. Crosses blazed on hillsides. Billboards reading "Nigger, don't let the sun set on you here" cast long shadows at town lines.

"I am the law in Indiana," crowed D. C. Stephenson, and for a short while he was. Months after the election he was convicted of kidnapping, molesting and murdering an Indianapolis woman. "Ed Jackson'll pardon me," he said, grinning, as they led him away. Twenty-five years later another governor did, on the condition that the sun never set on him again in Indiana.

Indiana's black population doubled between 1910 and 1930, as a steady stream of workers walked out of the cotton and tobacco fields of the South and sought work in the factories of Indianapolis and the Calumet cities of Gary, Hammond and East Chicago.

Whites clamored for segregated schools. The Indianapolis Chamber of Commerce called for a "separate, modern, completely equipped and adequate high school building for colored students." The Indiana Federation of Community Civic Clubs added that segregated schools—grade schools and high schools—would shield whites from the menace of tuberculosis, a disease which was slightly more prevalent among blacks at the time.

In December 1922 the Indianapolis school board recommended the construction of a high school for blacks. Citing the "laudable desire" of Negroes for a high school education, the board assured the city that the school would encourage their "self-reliance," "initiative" and "good citizenship."

The Klan-elected school board of 1925 was happy to keep the ball rolling by appropriating funds for construction. While the board members debated whether to name the school after Thomas Jefferson or Theodore Roosevelt, local black organizations, aided by the NAACP, filed lawsuits to stop construction of the school. They lost, and lost again on appeal. The school board decided that, if they felt that bad, maybe they should name the school themselves.

On September 12, 1927, the doors swung open to Crispus Attucks High School, named after the first black to die in the Revolutionary War. Thirteen hundred eighty-five students, kids uprooted from their neighborhood schools, filed into the classrooms, nearly double the number expected. The Ku Klux Klan organized several parades for the occasion. The Indianapolis *Star* reported that "One parade on Washington Street, consisting of row after row of masked Klansmen marching slowly to the beat of muffled drums, took an hour to pass." In this atmosphere, the black children of Indianapolis opened their books.

Until the late '40s most Indiana school officials would not have dreamed of allowing their athletes to play games against Crispus Attucks High School. Attucks' typical schedule for football and basketball consisted of a handful of games with the other two all-black Indiana schools— Gary Roosevelt and Evansville Lincoln—maybe a game with Indianapolis Cathedral, the Catholic school, and a few games with schools in Chicago, St. Louis, Dayton and Lexington.

Alonzo Watford, Attucks' athletic director from 1932 to 1957, was above all a resourceful man. At 5'4", 160 pounds, he had led the nation in scoring as a college football player at Butler University. In his playing days, when your knee touched the ground you could bounce back up and keep running. No one had ever found a way to keep Alonzo Watford down.

When he could talk someone into playing Attucks, it usually meant the expense of chartering a bus for a long trip. And everyone wanted the cash up front. Watford developed a network of angels, local black businesses and Butler alums who would stake him to a game. If he fell short, he'd get the students to sponsor bake sales. He was able to talk Butler into giving Attucks hand-me-down uniforms and shoes, which he then turned over to the tailoring and shoe repair shops as class projects.

Once he found out about a national high school football tournament in Tulsa, Oklahoma. He wrote to the sponsors and they said, sure, come on out. Watford quickly shook down all his angels, put $400 down for the bus, told the players to make sure they packed plenty of food—roadside restaurants that would welcome a large group of black teenagers were not abundant—and the Flying Tigers took off for the Wild West.

It started to snow in Missouri. They kept going until the driver couldn't see anymore. He pulled over. There they were, two coaches and two dozen black kids stranded in a bus in the middle of Kansas. Remarkably, they made the game—which they lost—turned around and came home.

The basketball team had an added burden. The Indiana High School Athletic Association (IHSAA) would not accept Attucks as a member school, and therefore Attucks couldn't play in the high school tournament. In the mid-'30s, the

IHSAA ruled that Attucks could play "contests [against member schools] in which not more than two schools should be involved at the same time," but the tournament was taboo.

It was terribly demoralizing. Some years Watford would find a game or two with some tiny rural school—Elletsville, Smithville and Paragon were the first—whose athletic directors were either daring or sympathetic—but then March would come, the whole state would be crazy with excitement and the Attucks kids would have to clean out their lockers and listen to everybody else on the radio.

Watford applied for IHSAA membership year after year, supported by the little member schools who had played Attucks. But the IHSAA was under no real pressure to relent; there were no black athletes in any of the major professional leagues at the time and few nonwhite players in college lineups.

In 1942 the IHSAA finally relented. But until then the reason IHSAA Secretary Arthur Trester gave Watford for not admitting Attucks was almost as insulting as the rejection itself. Trester told Watford, straight-faced, that Attucks was not a "public" school—as if Attucks were excluding someone who wanted in.

In all the long history of "Hoosier Hysteria," no Indianapolis school had ever won a state basketball championship. It was mortifying. It was hard for Indianapolis residents to face their out-of-town relatives for a couple of months after the tourney. Year after year, rural hecklers would call the Indianapolis sportswriters, get in a dig and hang up, cackling. The main reason was that kids in Indianapolis didn't know how to play basketball as well as their rural counterparts. Kids in most Indiana towns played organized ball with good coaches even in grade school. Indianapolis didn't start a grade school basketball program until 1951.

By the late '40s, the black kids of Indianapolis were starting to take to basketball. They flocked to the Indianapolis Coliseum whenever the Harlem Globetrotters came to town, and almost everyone had heard of Jumpin' Johnny Wilson, a 5'11" center who had led Anderson High to the 1946 state championship with his flying dunk shots.

Many of the best athletes came from the Lockfield Gardens, Indianapolis' first public housing project. Lockfield Gardens contained a slab of asphalt with netless hoops at either end that they all called the "Dust Bowl." It was the crucible for the best competition in the city, the kind of city game that is celebrated in the playgrounds of all major cities today.

Many of the players went to junior high school right next door to Attucks, at Public School 17, where in 1945 a math teacher named Ray Crowe started an intramural basketball program. In contrast to his players, Crowe knew "Hoosier Hysteria" firsthand. The eldest of eight boys in a family of ten children, Crowe had grown up on a farm and attended school in a small town south of Indianapolis. He'd grown up like white kids, playing on grade school teams and shooting at baskets on backboards nailed to barns.

The tough kids who poured into his intramural program loved him. He was short, stocky, handsome and tough. "He used to run up the wall, spring off it and slam-dunk," remembers Hallie Bryant, who now represents the Harlem Globetrotters. "That used to impress us little kids. He'd come into your neighborhood and take you to get a soda.

He'd visit your home and get to know your parents. He became like one of the family.

"He demanded respect, and he respected us. If he came in and said, 'Be quiet,' and you weren't quiet, he would shake you up. He wouldn't hurt guys or anything, but if they were cuttin' up he'd jack 'em up against the wall. He spoke very softly, but we figured he carried a real big stick."

In 1950 Crowe was asked to become Attucks' assistant coach. The next year the head coach resigned and Crowe was named to replace him. It was all very sudden. Having no high school coaching experience, Crowe hustled off to every camp and clinic he could find.

Crowe almost won the state tourney in his first year. Everything, even luck, seemed to be on Attucks' side. They won the semistate by beating Anderson High on a miraculous shot from the corner by Bailey ("Flap") Robertson. The ball hit the rim, bounded straight up and fell cleanly through at the buzzer. Attucks finally lost to Evansville Reitz in the afternoon round of the finals.

It was a monumental feat, achieved far too suddenly for many. There had been no time for anyone to get used to the notion of Attucks as a power. Crowe not only had to contend with whites who viewed the Attucks team as a potential vehicle for revolution, but also with Attucks' administrators, who feared the consequences of success.

"I would call the attitude 'defeatist,'" recalls Crowe of the mind set at Attucks when he arrived as coach. "It took some time for the principal to get adjusted to big-time athletics. He liked to come down and talk to the boys. He'd tell 'em not to be too rough, not to commit fouls, to be good sports. It was kind of a timid approach."

"They were total gentlemen," recalls Bob Collins, sports

editor of the Indianapolis *Star*, who covered Indianapolis basketball for the paper at the time. "They played the loosest zone you ever saw in your life. Every time the whistle blew, the Attucks player put up his hand because he knew it was gonna be against him."

The 1951 Attucks team galvanized black Indianapolis. "When Attucks would win," recalls Marcus Stewart, now the editor of the Indianapolis *Recorder*, "all black people would celebrate. Indiana Avenue would go wild. It was like when Joe Louis would whip someone."

One of Attucks' cheerleaders made up a song that rubbed the new order in everyone's faces. Called the "C-R-A-Z-Y" song, the Attucks fans, weaving back and forth en masse, would begin to sing it when the game was iced, just as Red Auerbach used to light his victory cigar. "Oh, Tech is rough/ And Tech is tough/They can beat everybody/But they can't beat us." The earlier the song was heard, the more delicious the goad.

In 1951 the tourney was televised for the first time, and the images of local heros entered homes and bars and department-store showrooms. No longer did black kids have to wait for the Globetrotters, for right there on the screen were Hallie Bryant and Willie Gardner and Flap Robertson, guys from Lockfield, from the Dust Bowl, from Attucks.

And Attucks had a new style, high, fast and flashy. They weren't interested in working the ball around for set shots. They ran hard all game long and made up shots to fit any occasion. They seemed to play the game above the rim. Attucks' center Willie Gardner—who the next year went straight from high school to the Harlem Globetrotters— was the first player many Hoosiers ever saw dunk the ball in a game.

Hallie Bryant (left) and Willie Gardner, two of Ray Crowe's early stars, ponder the future. Bryant enrolled at Indiana University and Gardner signed with the Harlem Globetrotters out of high school. *(Frank H. Fisse)*

The spoils of victory: Crispus Attucks's coach Ray Crowe anchors a kickline of cheerleaders. *(Courtesy Mary Oglesby)*

Crispus Attucks High flew away with basketball in Indiana. *(Indianapolis* Recorder *Collection, Indiana Historical Society)* (RIGHT)

Ku Klux Klan political rally, Muncie, Indiana, 1924, at a time when the Klan dominated Indiana politics. *(W. A. Swift Photo Collection, Bracken Library, Ball State University)*

An elated Oscar Robertson after controlling the 1955 title game: "Suddenly we were INDIANAPOLIS Crispus Attucks." *(Frank H. Fisse)* (RIGHT)

After the tourney, Ray Crowe spent a grim summer blaming himself for not winning the championship, for not making the kids play tougher, for letting them back off. He vowed not to let it happen again. "It was the way they had been brought up," he says. "They felt they shouldn't knock heads the way you have to if you're going to be a winner. I came up playin' against white kids. I went to school with 'em. I finally got my point across, but it took me years."

While Crowe agonized, Alonzo Watford was having the time of his life. The phone was ringing off the hook. Attucks had become box office. "Do you think you could find an opening sometime in February?" the athletic directors would ask politely. On top of that, they were offering whopping sums, hundreds of dollars, bus fares included.

Alonzo Watford recounted these events from a bed shortly before he died. Until he thought of those courteous phone calls, his face had been contorted with the labor of speech, of struggling to build words syllable by syllable. Then he began to chuckle, and soon laughter shook his frame. "Those people had never seen a Negro before," he said. "We were something unusual. One game with us could make the whole year for them. It got so I could play *Podunk* and make money." Tears of laughter rolled down Alonzo Watford's face. "Man, what a great feeling," he said.

Attucks could not escape the wicked Indianapolis sectional in 1952, but Ray Crowe saw something that year that looked like the ticket back to the state finals. Flap Robertson's younger brother Oscar, then an eighth grader at Public School 17, looked like he was going to be something.

Crowe watched the tall, skinny kid score half his team's points in leading P.S. 17 to the first Indianapolis grade

114

school championship. "He could shoot well and had all those moves and fakes," Crowe recalls. But at the end of each half, Oscar did something that impressed Crowe even more, just as it would impress fans for the next two decades. Very deliberately, Oscar dribbled the ball while the seconds ticked away, and then gave a couple of fakes and scored just before the buzzer. "He just *ran* the game," Crowe recalls.

Oscar Robertson was already well known at the Dust Bowl. At first, he had to play with the younger kids while it was still hot, before the big games started. But one summer he came back after a few months in Tennessee standing 6'3". He seemed eager to look up the kids who had put him down.

There was this sense of combat about him. Hallie Bryant remembers him at the Dust Bowl: "He was always challenging people. He was big for his age, but he had to gain the older guys' respect to get on the court. So he was always sayin', 'Get this, get this,' like, 'See if you can block this,' even to the guys with the big reputations."

Oscar started at forward his sophomore year, but Attucks' hopes were crushed in 1954 by Milan's team of destiny, a team from a rural school with 161 white kids. Milan gave Attucks the soundest beating of any team Ray Crowe had ever coached. Still, there was a sense that the guard was soon to change.

Early in 1955 it became clear that Oscar Robertson and Crispus Attucks High School were a special team, maybe a once-in-a-lifetime team. Everyone wanted to see them play. Seven of their first thirteen games had to be rescheduled, usually to a Tuesday or Wednesday night, and played in a gym big enough to hold the multitudes. One frosty weeknight, Attucks played Indianapolis Shortridge before

11,561 fans at Butler Field House. Local papers called it "possibly a world's record crowd for a non-tournament game." Attucks' share of the take for that game alone was $3,200. Before Oscar Robertson left Attucks, the athletic fund would swell to over $40,000, enough to finance printing presses and engineering equipment for the school. Watford could have chartered a bus to the moon.

Attucks no longer had to go out of Indiana to find games, but there were still no seats in their gym. Every game was an away game. Though they expected trouble on the road, it never came. Today, Attucks players and coaches remember the crowds as generous and the players as respectful. The officials were thought to be another matter.

Crowe and his players were convinced that referees would call any close call against Attucks. He told his players never to argue with the referees, but to assume they were playing against seven people. He told them to get ahead early and play like the game was tied the whole way, because he didn't want a close game at the end.

Attucks entered the 1955 tournament 21–1, having lost by only one point to Connersville. Attucks had no trouble in the tournament until they met Muncie Central in the semistate final. Muncie and Attucks had been rated first and second in Indiana all year long, and the game lived up to all expectations. With Attucks ahead 71–70 in the closing seconds, Oscar intercepted a pass and flung the ball high in the air as the buzzer sounded.

As the state finals approached, the white citizens of Indianapolis were forced to consider Crispus Attucks seriously. For many whites, Attucks was above all a mysterious place. Few whites even knew where the school was;

many, not knowing any better, called it "Christmas Attucks."

Black or white, these kids were in a position to do Indianapolis one immortal favor: win the tournament and end the nightmare. "People who had never talked to each other were talking to each other," says Collins. "Attucks was a common denominator." Oscar Robertson remembers, "Before we got to the state finals we were just known as 'Crispus Attucks.' But when we got into the finals we were suddenly *Indianapolis* Crispus Attucks."

But even in a thaw, the years of distance and ignorance between blacks and whites were formidable barriers. "The week before the finals, I got called into the superintendent's office," recalls then-Attucks Principal Dr. Russell A. Lane. "There were representatives from the mayor's office and from the police and fire departments. The mayor's man said, 'Well, looks like your boys are going to win next week.' I said, 'We think so.' He said, 'We're afraid if they do, your people will break up the city and tear down all the lampposts.' I said, 'There will not be one incident.' "

Dr. Lane spent much of the next week advising students to restrain themselves even in celebration. A car turned over in jubilation, he explained to them, might well be held against everyone as evidence of the Negro's violent nature.

It turned out to be an all-black final game, Attucks vs. Gary Roosevelt, which made rooting for Attucks much easier for many Indianapolis whites. Roosevelt had a fine team, including Dick Barnett, who was later to star for the New York Knicks, but they were hopelessly undermatched. Attucks demolished them 97–64, scoring twenty-nine points more than any team had ever scored in a final tournament game.

Oscar Robertson was a man among boys, scoring thirty

points and tossing soft lead passes to teammates Willie Merriweather and Sheddrick Mitchell for flying layups. His movements were smooth and purposeful, his knowledge seemed ancient. If there was no fast break, Oscar bounced the ball up the floor, froze his defender with a little fake or two and then dispatched him as clinically as possible. Thirty years later, he remarked, characteristically, that he had never dunked in a game.

After the game, the Attucks players, coaches and administrators were carried in fire trucks around the Indianapolis Monument Circle, a traditional honor for Indianapolis sectional winners. Thousands of Indianapolis citizens, blacks and whites, found themselves mingling together—many for the first time ever—lost in the rapture of winning.

The players and coaches rode shoulder-to-shoulder with the city officials who had a few days before cautioned restraint in such a setting. It was hard for them to feel uninhibited. "For a team that had just won a state championship," recalls Oscar Robertson, "that was the most orderly group of people you ever saw."

Then the fire trucks turned north and headed through the black community, through the slums, down Indiana Avenue to Northwestern Park, away from the downtown area. They drove to Northwestern Park, where a crowd of 25,000—much of Indianapolis' black community—was waiting for the team. A bonfire blazed and speakers blared out popular favorites like "Kokomo" and "Tweedle Dee." The "C-R-A-Z-Y" song was sung enough to last until the next winter.

Some blacks took the parade route, out of downtown Indianapolis and into the black neighborhoods, to be an act of rejection. Oscar Robertson is one of them. "I remember he came home early that night," says Oscar's father, Henry, "about 10:30. He got a sandwich and lay down on the living room floor. He said, 'Dad, they really don't want us,' and went to bed." He has not changed his mind about the parade. "It's disgusting that they'd mess with the minds of 16- and 17-year-old kids like that," says Oscar.

"That parade was the shame of the city," says Bob Collins. "It was just a lack of feeling and understanding. Whites thought it'd be nice to give blacks a parade through their own neighborhoods, so they could celebrate. There was a total white misunderstanding of blacks. That in itself is a form of prejudice."

But a lot of black Hoosiers were too elated to think about the parade route. "That was the happiest day in the lives of a whole generation of black people," says Marcus Stewart. "I danced all night. At last we had something to be proud of. Attucks was *ours.*"

Indianapolis had instituted a neighborhood school plan of sorts in 1949, wiping out a century-old law entitling a public education to all but "persons of color." But two giant loopholes made it all but meaningless: white students were granted transfers out of the almost all-black Attucks neighborhood, and all black students in Indianapolis were allowed to "cross their line" and go to Attucks. Some of the most talented athletes did so, to play basketball for Ray Crowe.

"The success of Attucks' basketball integrated the high schools of Indianapolis," says Bob Collins. "They became so dominant that the other schools had to get black basketball players or forget about it.

"They [the other schools] went from not caring to crying

'unfair.' They were even saying, this is *illegal*. They were saying, 'Oscar lives in the Shortridge district, and Hallie Bryant should be goin' to Tech.' In 1951, I don't think any other team in Marion County had a black player. By 1955, Shortridge had four black starters." For his part, Dr. Lane says simply, "Things got a lot better for blacks around here after those teams."

Today, Crispus Attucks High School stands as sort of an island, not so much out of place as devoid of any context whatsoever. The marbled columns flanking the front door now face an entrance ramp to Interstate 65, which a few years ago shattered the neighborhood.

To the south, through a hurricane fence topped by three strands of barbed wire, there is an abandoned shopping center. A hospital and a university have gobbled up blocks of single-family houses. The Lockfield Gardens Projects have been condemned for destruction. Last year, despite desperate efforts by black and historic organizations, P.S. 17, where Ray Crowe started it all, gave way to the wrecker's ball and collapsed in a heap of rubble. There is now an initiative to make Attucks a junior high. Within Indianapolis' black community there is a general sense that, as the local university campus expands, Attucks itself is not long for this world.

"If I could have looked ahead when I was in high school and found out that someday I'd get to coach at Crispus Attucks High School, I probably would have fainted," says Larry Humes, Attucks' basketball coach since 1977.

But it's not the same. In 1969, the Indianapolis schools were finally integrated after a federal court found the Indianapolis school board guilty of *de jure* segregation and installed a busing plan. Many of the good local athletes are bused to the suburbs nowadays, and there are no grade schools left to feed Humes the stars of the future.

Alonzo Watford's mighty athletic fund shriveled to ninety dollars at one point in 1980. Ray Crowe, who retired from coaching in 1958 and later served six terms in the Indiana legislature, finds it frustrating to watch the games. "I go to the games now and see these little puny kids . . . they just don't *look* like basketball players," he says.

Crispus Attucks High graduated its first integrated class in 1974. Though the school is one-third white now, its halls are still lined with the class photos of three generations of black Indianapolis, composites of parents and aunts and uncles and cousins.

If walls could talk, Attucks' would be worth listening to. They'd know the "C-R-A-Z-Y" song for sure. Those walls could tell good stories, old-fashioned stories with heroes and villains and morals at the end. The halls could shout and cry and ring with laughter. It may be that more than any other building, Crispus Attucks High School has known Hoosiers at their best and worst.

THE MOUNTS:

Lebanon's
First Family

In the late '60s a drive up Highway 52 from Indianapolis or down from Chicago took you through Lebanon, Indiana, population 9,500. At the town line, right beside the rack of service club emblems, the Lions and the Elks and the Rotary and the Kiwanis, draped there like medals on a general's breast, a second sign stood taller and truer. It read, "Lebanon, Indiana, Home of Rick Mount, Mr. Basketball 1966."

The biography of that roadside sign tells us the story of Rick Mount's basketball days. Erected after his senior year in high school as a monument to the most publicized career in the history of Indiana basketball, the sign was ripped from the highway by a jubilant mob and carried thirty-five miles up the road to West Lafayette after Mount's jump shot gave Purdue University a tournament win in 1969. Hours later, Lebanon police roared up, recaptured it and returned it tenderly to its natural habitat. Several years later, after Mount's professional career had fizzled to a premature conclusion, the sign was discreetly removed.

But the sign tells only part of the story, a third to be exact, for it could just as easily have been planted there to commemorate the feats of Rick's father, Pete, as a way of marking the town for the Studebakers and Packards flying by at a mile a minute, and it may well rise again to celebrate the tenure of his gifted son, Richie.

This is the story of three generations of a family which has lived in the same small town, gone to the same school and whose males have been the main producers of their town's principal export—points. Adored and celebrated, the Mounts have lived in what Rick has described as "a little shell," a world in which, given the adulation they have received, it has seemed enough to be able to throw a ball through an iron ring better than anyone else in town, or Indiana, or in Rick's case maybe the world.

But something happened in 1985 that tested the strength of the shell. Rick and his wife Donna allowed their son Richie to repeat the eighth grade, mainly in order to give Richie another year to develop as a basketball player; to use a phrase more commonly heard around college gyms, they "red-shirted" Richie. To the Mounts this was not a moral issue, it was a gift to their son of a year's time. Plenty of other people they knew had done the same thing.

But Richie is the son of the man whom many have called "the greatest pure shooter of all time," and, when the word got out, Rick was back in the headlines again, cast this time not as a hero but as a man whose values required inspection and realignment. Rick found more than a little irony in all this: he and his dad had both repeated a grade, and there hadn't been too many complaints back then, when they were putting Lebanon on the map. The story of the Mounts of Lebanon is, as much as anything, the story of a changing Indiana.

Lebanon is the seat of Boone County, a horizon of corn and soybean fields broken by groves of beech and maple, by farmsteads, ranch houses and small towns. Back down the gravel roads, past flagged mailboxes, where dogs give your tires a tiny head start, a few of the barns still have "Chew Mail Pouch" painted on the side, only now beginning to fade.

Boone County was established by an act of the 1830 Indiana legislature. It followed that there had to be a county seat, so the governor appointed five commissioners to go out there and find one and give it a name. An early account describes their quest:

Three of them met near the center of the county on about May 1, 1831. They were required by law to locate the seat within two miles of the center of the county. They finally chose a tall, dense forest where no one lived, not even Indians. They drove a large stake in the ground where the courthouse now stands. But they couldn't agree on a name for the town.

Mr. A. M. French, the youngest of the commissioners, lay nearby, quietly sleeping, unconcerned by what the name might be. He was aroused and told that the others had failed and had left the name solely up to him. He gazed up at the tall trees around him, and he thought of the tall cedars of Lebanon in sacred history—he thought of the River Jordan—here were the tall trees, a little way off was Prairie Creek; thus the name was evolved in his mind—he shouted "Lebanon!" The name was fixed. Lebanon it has henceforth been.

Lebanon is within an area of perhaps a thirty-mile radius that was Indiana's first basketball hotbed. Schools from within this area won the first eight Indiana high school basketball tournaments. In 1911, the Lebanon High School Tigers finished second to despised Crawfordsville in the first tournament but then won three of the next seven. Lebanon can stake some claim to being Indiana's first real basketball power.

Those vintage teams played their home games in the second floor of a hotel, in a small square room with a pot-bellied stove in the corner and a few hundred seats around the court. The instant the doors were opened, townspeople stampeded in out of the cold, stomped and brushed the snow off, and huddled together until the room became warm enough for shirt sleeves and coveralls. Outside, a house painter named Tom Dawson steadied his ladder against the building and stood in the dark on the top rung, nose pressed flat against the window, swaying in the winter wind.

John Mount came to Lebanon from Kentucky around the turn of the century. He tried his hand at farming for a while, then found a better living pouring cement and smoothing out the streets and sidewalks of the growing town. Like nearly every other male in Lebanon, John lived for Friday nights. When he had sons of his own, he walked them to the gym and told them he wished he could afford a car to follow the Tigers on the road.

Pete Mount, born in 1926, remembers walking to the games from the first grade on. "You didn't want to sit too close to my dad in a close game," Pete recalls. "You were liable to get a rib full of his elbow all night." Young Pete was there the night the Zionsville fan went at the referee with a whiskey bottle. Sometimes when arch-foe Frankfort came to town, the fighting began in the runway to the dressing rooms and spilled outside into the parking lot. It was most exciting when big teams like Lafayette Jefferson and Muncie Central came through. He loved to sit around afterwards with his dad and hear Doc Porter and Butch Neuman and the others tell the stories of the old teams, when it was *really* tough. He wanted to be a Tiger.

He grew up tall for the times, 6'1", skinny at 145 pounds, but a terrific shooter, the kind who could always find the basket even through a tangle of arms. Pete played constantly, shooting at peanut cans and goals nailed to barns and garages and telephone poles. For one thing, he says, there really wasn't much else to do.

When the time came, Pete started on the Lebanon High basketball varsity as a freshman, a rare privilege granted historically only to a precocious few. Given his slender build, it helped that he was a bit old for a freshman, having repeated the second semester of third grade. To maintain turf, Pete found he had to "let an elbow slip every now and then."

Pete broke all the scoring records at Lebanon and almost led the Tigers to the state championship. In Pete's junior year, 1943, Lebanon got to the championship game for the first time since 1918 but lost by five points to Fort Wayne Central. For his effort, the Indianapolis *Star* named Pete "Star of Stars" for the 1943 state tournament.

Pete knew he would never have another chance. There was a war on, and Pete had to report for duty on March 1, 1944, which fell before the state finals. As it turned out, Lebanon was upset in the sectionals anyway—and off to war he went.

You don't find a lot of foxholes and shells in Pete's war stories: When he reported to Fort Harrison, he learned that his sergeant had already signed him up for a basketball tournament in Indianapolis. He played in California, then at Fort Riley, Kansas, then at Fort Sill, Oklahoma. "I set the scoring record there, forty-three points in one game," recalls Pete. "No, I think some guy tied it just before I left."

They shipped Pete's unit to Germany, but the war in Europe had ended by the time he got there. They were sent home for thirty days to rest up for the final assault on Japan. While he was in Lebanon, Pete married his high school sweetheart, Katie McLain, with whom he had gone steady since he was a freshman. A few days later Pete was with his unit, ready to leave, when they heard that something called the atomic bomb had changed their schedule again.

In April 1946 Pete was discharged. He and Katie took the Pullman together from Fort Jackson, South Carolina, to Indianapolis, with plenty to talk about. Teams of all kinds were tugging at Pete. Indiana, Purdue and Clemson wanted him to play college basketball. The Indianapolis Indians wanted him to play minor league baseball.

Pete began the summer laying cement with his dad. Butch Neuman, his old coach, hounded Pete to stay near home and go to college at Purdue. But Katie was pregnant, and the couple needed money. One day when Butch happened to be out of town, Doxie Moore, coach of the Sheboygan Redskins of the new Basketball Association of America—a forerunner of the NBA—came through and offered Pete a contract. Pete wasn't sure, but Doxie Moore— he later became lieutenant governor of Indiana—was a persuasive man. He offered Pete no bonus but a $1,500 salary, plus more for exhibition games. It sounded like a fortune. When Butch returned, Pete was gone.

It was a mistake from the start. Pete had always been a center, but now he had to play guard. He had to learn to shoot facing the basket, to set and twirl up a two-handed set. Almost everyone in the league was bigger and more experienced. His loose elbows underneath didn't faze the likes of George Mikan. Pete was released at the end of the season and went back home to Lebanon. Anyway, it was time to quit fooling around; Pete and Katie had a son.

If ever a boy was born to score baskets, it was Rick Mount. As if it weren't enough to be Pete's son, the hands that pulled him into the world and whacked the breath of life into him belonged to Richard Porter, the very same hands that had scored twenty-six points for the Tigers in the 1912 state championship game; it took more than thirty years for anyone else to score more in a final game. It was as if all the forces of the town's history had gathered on that day to produce a marksman.

Pete started the boy out with a peanut can, just like the one he'd had, cut out at the bottom, supporting a string net dipped in wax. When Rick got bigger, Pete nailed a goal to the garage. After Pete would come home from his job tracking down airplane engine parts and delivering them from plant to plant at a division of General Motors in Indianapolis, he'd wash up and find Rick out back.

Their shooting contests would turn into games, and Pete didn't give anything away. "It'd make him mad 'cause he couldn't win," Pete says. "He'd drive under the goal sometimes, and I'd say, 'No, you're not going to get that baseline on me,' and I'd put him up against the garage door and he'd quit doin' that. He'd keep movin' back, of course, but I could shoot farther with my two-handed set. But then he started stoppin', and jumpin' and poppin' 'em on me, you know."

Those who lived in central Indiana at the time began to hear stories about Rick Mount when he was in junior high. It was as if another Mozart had been discovered in a cornfield. Hundreds of people followed Rick's fifth- and sixth-grade teams all over Boone County, just to watch the boy play.

Jim Rosenstihl became the Lebanon varsity coach during Rick's eighth-grade year. "Rosey," as everyone called him, and Pete were longtime friends, having played against each other in high school. Rosey's first chance to see Pete's kid for himself came in a summer league he set up for his seventh- and eighth-graders—forty games on sweltering asphalt from mid-May through August. As he often put it, a kid whose desire wilts in hot weather is not the kid you want with the ball in his hands for the Lebanon Tigers with a game on the line.

The boy was an unbelievable natural jump-shooter. He must have learned it on his own, too, Rosey thought, because Pete had never learned to shoot a jump shot. There is an episode repeated in Hoosier folklore—one could liken it, maybe, to the adolescent Jesus educating the elders—where Rosey took Rick, still an eighth-grader, to a shooting clinic at a statewide coaches' conference. At one point, Rosey trotted Rick out to demonstrate the "minute drill." Before more than a hundred astonished coaches, the boy drilled twenty of twenty-two long-distance jump shots within a minute.

When the Lebanon High School season began, Rosey started Rick on the varsity as a freshman, just as Pete had started a quarter-century before. Like Pete, Rick was a year older than the others in his class, having repeated second grade. Rick averaged over twenty points a game and quickly began to receive statewide attention.

Part of Rick's appeal was the way he looked. He was long and lean, perfect in a pair of pegged jeans, with killer blue eyes and high cheekbones. He had a sense of style. His blond hair was customized into a curl that hung onto his forehead. He wore his collars and sleeves up.

He grew to be 6′4″, tall enough to be a high school center, but his was an outside game. He could shoot left-handed or right, and with players hanging all over him. He would dribble the ball at high speed, bounce it hard a final time and leap, delivering the ball at the height of his jump. He always seemed able to jump straight up, no matter how fast he was running.

Rick Mount's jump shot came to be to small-town Hoosierland what Earl Monroe's spins or Julius Erving's dunks were to the cities: a perfect visual expression of the experience. There were long flat spaces and seasons and thunderstorms in Rick's jumper. A film wouldn't do it justice, it was a shot to be canned and preserved. The delivery was easy and light, the balance and trajectory sure and beautiful. Suddenly it seemed that all the great shooters of Indiana's history had done it wrong, but there had been no way of knowing this until someone did it right.

Jim Rosenstihl and Rick Mount were a match made in heaven, like Elvis and the Colonel. Rick was prodigiously talented, and Rosey, handsome, slow-talking, tireless, shrewd and genuinely in love with basketball, is one of the great promoters in the history of the high school game in Indiana. Lebanon was winning games, and Rosey had the centerpiece of the state. Letters from colleges were pouring in, including a feeler from Tuskegee Institute.

Between Rick's sophomore and junior years, Miami University coach Bruce Hale turned up in Lebanon with one Aldo Leone of New York City, a gentleman who said he was the nephew of a famous Manhattan restaurateur named Mama Leone. He said he knew pretty near every basketball

coach and player in the New York City high school world—
they called it "the prep scene" out there.

One of Aldo's friends was Jack Donahue, the coach at
Power Memorial High School, who had a towering young
center named Lew Alcindor. Rosey and Aldo started ban-
tering about who would win a dream game between Rick
the Rocket from the Hoosier cornfields and the next Wilt.
Aldo said he'd get the game started, and damned if Donahoe
didn't call soon.

They agreed to try it in Indianapolis, where the crowds
would surely be big. Donahue made Rosey promise to send
clippings of the pregame hype. He said the New York papers printed only the high school scores, and to him the
coverage looked like the obituary section.

They almost pulled it off. Tickets were printed, Butler
Field House was rented, there were oceans of ink in the
papers—and then the Indiana High School Athletic Association abruptly backed out, claiming the game would have
been billed as a "national championship." To this day, Rosey thinks Lebanon would have won.

Rick's world at the time was circumscribed by the
boundaries of his hometown. He had rarely been outside
of Indiana, and he spent almost all his time with his teammates, coaches, hunting pals and the downtown merchants
who sought to bask in his spreading fame. He had no brothers or sisters; probably his best friend was his special girl
since early grade school, Donna Cadger.

Pete and Katie's marriage came apart before Rick's freshman year, and Pete moved out. Despite all the hours of
games, Rick and Pete were not close at the time. "He never

would let me come to his junior high games," recalls Pete. "I think he was afraid I'd start yelling and make a scene." "I didn't really know my dad," says Rick. "I looked at his scrapbooks, but it wasn't till I got older that people told me how good he was. I don't know why he didn't tell me. Maybe he didn't want to put any added pressure on me."

Rick seemed shy, withdrawn and often aloof to those outside his circle. He felt everyone's eyes upon him. "It's like you're in a little glass and everyone's peeking in at you," Rick recalls. "Anything I would do, people would say, 'Oh, that's terrible,' or 'That's okay.' It makes you kind of a loner. People don't know what to say to you and they walk up to you and say something smart. You don't even know them, they think it's funny but they don't know what to say to you and you think they are being a smart aleck or something. You just kind of get turned off."

Rick's summer habitat was an outdoor court in Lebanon Park, a couple of hundred yards from a pool where he worked as a lifeguard. Every few hours he'd whistle everyone out of the pool, drop down from the tower, pull on his sneakers and head for the court. "Hey, kid," he'd say to one of the boys who hung around him, "want an ice cream cone? Rebound a hundred shots and I'll buy you one."

Nights and weekends were for games. As his reputation grew, more and more players, especially black kids from Indianapolis, drove out to try their luck. Though they invited him to the city, Rosey kept Rick on his own court, and the rules were shooter's rules. At Lebanon Park the offensive player called the fouls.

Saturday night was date night. But if Rick had a date, he'd always drive past the court. "I remember once a date and I drove by the court on the way to the drive-in and I saw five or six black players out there. I didn't know them.

134

I looked out there and thought, hey, those guys are pretty good. So I told the girl, 'I got to take you home.' I took her home and she got out of the car and slammed the door. I got home real quick and got my shoes and went back. I never had another date with her but I got in some good games. How many guys would do that?"

Few Hoosiers who have become famous have made their mark in Indiana. Abraham Lincoln, who spent his youth in southern Indiana, made it big in Illinois and Washington, Michael Jackson in California, James Dean, Cole Porter and Hoagy Carmichael in New York. Maybe only Wendell Wilkie's presidential candidacy, Larry Bird's senior year in Terre Haute and Eugene Debs at the peak of his fame could rival the notoriety Rick Mount received as a senior in high school and a collegian at Purdue.

One event changed Rick's—and Lebanon's—life by thrusting them both into the national spotlight. Midway through Rick's senior year, Rosey got a call from Frank DeFord, a writer for *Sports Illustrated*, inquiring about a story on Rick. Never one to shy away from publicity, Rosey said, "Come on out," and soon DeFord and photographer Rich Clarkson were part of the family.

To hear Rosey and Rick tell it today, Lebanon was like a movie set for two weeks. DeFord and Clarkson followed Rick everywhere, Clarkson snapping hundreds of pictures in the classroom, in the gym, in the town square. Rick says that once he saw Clarkson behind him as he entered the restroom at school. He turned around. "Anywhere but in here," he said.

"One of the shots they wanted to take, I don't know why, was with Rick downtown and by the poolroom," says Rosey.

"He was standin' right out in the middle of the street with cars comin' by. I was standin' down on one end of the street makin' sure no one ran over him and DeFord was on the other end. Suddenly Pistol Sheets, the guy who owns the poolroom, came runnin' outside, wavin' a gun around, yellin', 'I'll shoot the first guy that hits him!' "

On February 14, 1966, the town merchants gathered around the delivery truck that pulled up in front of the drugstore and tore at the string that bound the magazines. There was Rick on the *cover*, profiled from the waist up against a farmhouse, wearing his Lebanon High warm-up jacket, his lips parted in what appeared to be a bashful smile, his patented curl in place. It was the first time a high school basketball player had ever appeared on the cover of *Sports Illustrated*.

They devoured the article. Rick was declared maybe the best high school player of all time, as good as Oscar Robertson was. Well, fair enough, exept maybe for the Oscar part. That was still debatable. He was said to possess the moves of a cat, the eyes of a hawk and the presence of a king. That sounded about right. On the other hand, they felt *they* came off as hicks, which still leaves a bad taste in Lebanon when you bring the article up. For his part, Rick, while suitably honored, wished maybe they could have left Oscar, his ultimate hero, out of it.

The state tournament started the following weekend. As usual, Lebanon easily won the sectional and regional tourneys, but they began the afternoon game of the semistate heavy underdogs, billed as a one-man team against a tough Logansport squad.

No one who saw it will ever forget the Logansport game. Down 51–39 with eight minutes left, Rick decided he was at least going to go down shooting. He scored twenty points

The best of times: Rick Mount as a Lebanon High star,
with his coach Jim "Rosey" Rosenstihl. *(Courtesy Jim Rosenstihl)*

Richie Mount, Pete Mount and Jim Rosenstihl, mid-
1970s, after a Lebanon Tigers game. *(Courtesy Pete Mount)*

(LEFT)

Rick Mount, the pure jump-shooter, 1966. *(Courtesy Jim Rosenstihl)*

Richie Mount puts a move on his dad, 1985. *(Shoshana Hoose)*

in those minutes, hitting seven bombs in a row in one immortal stretch. When the smoke cleared, Lebanon had won by a point, and Rick had scored forty-seven of his team's sixty-five points. Leg cramps destroyed Rick in the night game—just as cramps had sidelined his father in the tourney—and Lebanon lost by a single point.

The following morning, sports editor John Whittaker wrote in the Hammond *Times*: "I've seen a few great things in my time. I was there when Red Grange went wild against Michigan. I saw the famous Dempsey-Tunney title fight. I watched the Babe call his home run shot . . . and now this performance by Mount."

When the headlines appeared announcing that Rick Mount had signed a letter of intent to attend the University of Miami, the people of Lebanon, and Indiana, were stunned. "People on the street wouldn't even speak to me," says Rick.

Given the reaction, Rosey advised Rick that, just to be safe, maybe he'd better also sign a letter of intent with a Big Ten school. Before long, Rick told Bruce Hale he had changed his mind and signed with Purdue. Lebanon was jubilant. One of every nine residents—including infants and the elderly—bought season tickets to Purdue's schedule in Rick's first year.

West Lafayette, Indiana, home of Purdue University, is just thirty miles from Lebanon. Rick never really took to college life; he didn't grow up dreaming of life as a Fiji or a Deke. His girlfriend, Donna, was enrolled, too, and soon they were married and living in student housing, driving back to Lebanon on nongame weekends.

Lebanon never seemed to change. The downtowners

were always coming up with some crazy scheme. There was still the sign with Rick's name on it at the town line, and now there was a life-size cardboard cutout of himself in uniform at the bank. The court at Lebanon Park had been dedicated to Rick, with a sign of course, and Rosey now had a booklet out about jump-shooting which featured the shooting statistics of every game Rick had played in.

Purdue coach George King built an offense around Rick, with his big men leaping out like muggers to set picks. That was fine with Rick, just like Lebanon. And Purdue had real talent. Bill Keller and Herman Gilliam, both of whom later had fine professional careers, kept the defenses honest and set up the plays.

Rick was an even better collegian than a high school player. Three times he was an All-American, and, as a senior, he averaged about forty points per game in the Big Ten Conference. Such scoring was unheard-of. It was then that Al McGuire, John Havlicek and others started calling Rick the best "pure shooter" they had ever seen. For some reason, when you saw Rick Mount shoot, there was no need to explain what an impure shooter was.

The best night of his college career came as a junior in the NCAA Mideast Regionals against Marquette. Purdue, an underdog, found itself a point down and with the ball in the closing seconds. George King set up the obvious play, and it couldn't have worked better. Rick got the ball, drove his man through one deadening pick and into another and found himself sky-blue free in the corner with four seconds left. He swished his jumper, and Purdue was off to the finals.

It was after that intoxicating game that Purdue fans carried his highway sign from Lebanon up to West Lafayette and transplanted it near a fountain on a campus hill. Maybe on that night, too, Rick Mount, like his billboard, was liberated from Lebanon.

In the spring, after UCLA had throttled Purdue in the NCAA finals, the pros came, just as they had come for his dad. This time the money was a little better. There was a bidding war on between the NBA and the newly formed ABA. Rick signed with the Indiana Pacers for about a million dollars, chopped up into various investment schemes designed to make Rick financially secure forever.

At the time it was one of the biggest contracts ever. A physical education major, twenty-six credits shy of graduating, Rick quit school. He explained to the press that he had gone to college not to learn to be a tennis coach but to play pro basketball.

Rick's pro career turned out to be every bit the disappointment Pete's had been, in part because the expectations had been so high. It took five years for the end to come. The Indiana Pacers were a strong team whose offense was concentrated in the front court. For the first time in his life, Rick was not the center of the offense. Very few plays were set up for him. Often he wasn't a starter.

His confidence faded. He became convinced that his coach, Bobby Leonard, was out to ruin him. He badgered Leonard to trade him, and finally Mike Storen, the man who had signed him from Purdue, got him traded to Dallas and then on to Kentucky. There was one more trade, to the Utah Stars. When the Utah franchise's bankruptcy was announced, Rick was offered $16,000 for his fabled investment plan, into which few contributions had been made. He lost about $122,000.

The end had come too soon. He was 28 years old, a man

who had devoted his life to a single pursuit and who could do it as well as anyone else. It was hard to understand or accept. Like his dad, he went back to Lebanon. He too had a son.

"There was a big void in my life after I got out of basketball," says Rick. "You think to yourself, 'No more organized competition.' Boy, it's an empty feeling for a long time."

Rick and Donna Mount have remained in Lebanon. Both extended families are there, and they prefer a small-town atmosphere. Rick invested some of his Utah settlement in a sporting goods shop that went under after a few years. Since then, Rick has sold various athletic products and taught jump shooting at camps and clinics, while Donna has held a job at the pharmacy.

Rick was once offered a head coaching job at a Lafayette high school, but his decision to leave college early came back to haunt him when the IHSAA disqualified his contract. He talked to Purdue officials about making up the credits but came home discouraged.

Probably because he is so easy to find, as always in Lebanon, he is a target for schemes of varying promise. One entrepreneur envisions Rick as the figurehead for a series of basketball "Parlors"—gyms rented out like racquetball courts for the young professionals of Indianapolis. A filmmaker from Chicago says he's interested in basing a project on Rick's life story: "It's a guy from a small town that makes good and has some bad times," says Rick. "It's gonna be real educational. The guy was never into drugs and never smoked. The All-American boy."

Rick loves to work with young players. He can teach

almost anyone to shoot, adjusting an elbow here, shortening the stroke there, making sure the guide hand falls away so the shooter doesn't end up "thumbing" the ball. "I'm 38 years old and these kids still know Rick Mount because their dad told them," he says. "It really gives me a thrill if I can help kids shoot the basketball and get confidence in themselves."

Along with all the regular students, there has also been an apprentice. Rick started his son, Richie, with the traditional family peanut can, and through the years Rick has passed on to Richie the refinements of the guide hand and the planted foot, the subtleties of backspin and arch.

Rick has had more free time to work with Richie than Pete had for Rick, and there is far more structure to this apprenticeship. The project consumes them both. They work together constantly, and they work hard. It is as if a shooter is being bred.

Some kids might have rebelled at the regimen, but Richie can't get enough; the bond between the two is clearly loving and powerful. At 14, Richie Mount stands an inch under 6'. He's blonde with bangs, doe-eyed, respectful and shy.

On a summer afternoon before Richie's freshman year, the two worked out together in the driveway of the Mount's rented house on the north end of town. Richie wore a T-shirt that said "Rocket"—Rick's old nickname. A flatbed truck in the oversized driveway bore the sticker "Never Mind the Gun, Beware of the Owner." On the basketball goal, facing out onto a cornfield, the word "Mount" was painted in blue above the rim.

They began with a shooting drill. Rick led Richie with bounce passes, back and forth, around a perimeter eighteen feet from the basket. Richie's form is not like Rick's, in part because he's not yet strong enough to generate Rick's power. But the quick delivery off the dribble is there, and the result is the same. Richie hit his first seven shots.

The game shifted to one-on-one, with Rick carrying on a running commentary as they played. Rick crouched behind the foul circle, holding the ball low and in front of him, faked quickly and started to leap for his shot. Richie slapped the ball, causing Rick to miss badly. "He's playin' my shot," muttered Rick. "He knows what I'm going to do 'cause it's me." Rick returned the favor when Richie got the ball, slapping it loose. Richie's mouth formed a tight line. "He doesn't like it when I play him rough," said Rick, "but he's got to get over that 'cause I can teach him a lot. He doesn't like to lose."

In the summer of 1984 the Mounts decided to hold Richie back a year in school. "There are four reasons," says Rick. "It gives him an extra year of maturity. It helps his schoolwork. It helps him mentally, 'cause he's my kid and he's probably feeling a lot of pressure. I had more publicity than my dad did, and now there's more emphasis on athletics. And it'll help him get a college education, an athletic scholarship."

The Mounts reasoned that the extra year had helped Richie's dad and granddad, so why deprive Richie of the same chance? But Richie's situation was somewhat different. Both Rick and Pete had repeated a year in early grade school, and both had been at best average students. They had not decided to do it, it had just worked out that way. Richie was a good student, and this was a deliberate family decision.

That summer, Rick tried to figure out exactly how you

would arrange to have a kid repeat a grade. For a while, Rick thought he might have to pay to put Richie in a private church academy, for he assumed the middle school principal at Lebanon would resist. But then he talked to friends who, as eighth-graders at Lebanon, had gone to school in Indianapolis for a couple of months and then returned to Lebanon and were allowed to repeat eighth grade.

So the Mounts followed the traditional procedure. Richie started his second year of eighth grade in Connecticut and returned home about two months later. Rick took Richie into the principal's office and tried to enroll Richie as an eighth-grader. The principal refused. So the Mounts hired a lawyer and took their case to the school board. This has been going on for years, they said, why pick on our kid? Indeed, Rosey can cite seven kids who'd stayed an extra year at Lebanon during his twenty-three-year coaching career, and everyone knew of kids who had repeated grades for basketball in other Indiana towns.

By a 3–2 vote, in a packed and emotional hearing, the board granted the Mounts' request, citing the absence of a statute or policy forbidding such a move. The state educational bureaucracy asked the Lebanon board to reconsider, but the board held firm. Several months later, the IHSAA ordered schools to draw up rules and penalties against red-shirting in high school.

Rick Mount was news again. The school board's decision was featured on the front page of the Indianapolis *Star*. Television cameras rolled in for Richie's eighth-grade games. The Lebanon *Reporter*, the local newspaper, backed the Mounts editorially, again citing the absence of policy, and published about a week's worth of letters—mostly unsigned—before announcing a moratorium on Richie Mount mail. Excerpts from some of them show the depth of feeling in Lebanon:

It absolutely amazes me that in our society it has become acceptable for parents to consider the primary function of going to school to be the enhancement of their child's athletic abilities. . . . As a graduate of Lebanon High School, I am utterly embarrassed.

I wonder why the practice is so wrong all of a sudden. Is it red-shirting that is wrong suddenly or is it wrong now because it involves a youngster named Mount?

I have known Rick, Donna and Richie Mount for many years. They are basically good people, very interested in their son's well-being.

Is it fair that Richie gets this whole year to mature when almost every other basketball player does not? And if it is fair, who makes the decisions on which player can repeat eighth grade and which cannot? What if every eighth-grader did this . . . would anybody ever graduate from Lebanon?

"We had about a month of TV and radio call-in shows," says Rick. "People were callin' in and bad-mouthin' me. People were comin' up to me and sayin', 'Now you listen to this,' and I said, 'It's over with, it's my business and my family's business and it's over with.' It was a good experience for [Richie]. It shows you what people can be like."

This experience has, if anything, heightened Rick's sense of estrangement from his neighbors. He believes, and probably with good reason, that had Richie been anyone else's son, or had Richie had belonged to an earlier generation, the people of Lebanon would not have noticed, let alone held the family in judgment. "What's so funny is," he says, "bringing fame to this town brought more resentment toward me than happiness toward me from people in this town. I don't know why, but, you know, the more publicity you get, the more jealousy and contempt it brings."

Rosey's still the head coach at Lebanon High, slowed down by some health problems but, at 59, hoping he can coach for all of Richie's years. Pete, now retired, still lives in town. On summer afternoons when the Cubs aren't on TV, Pete drives over to the school to have lunch with Rosey in the cafeteria. Then they stroll back to Rosey's office— the authentic seat of Boone County—and visit for an hour or two.

If you prod, you can get Pete and Rosey to give their opinions on Richie's grade repetition. Pete says it goes on all the time, so what's the fuss? Rosey says it just boils down to a year out of a person's earning life, a sacrifice a kid has a right to make if he wants to. Both agree that if Richie weren't Rick Mount's kid, no one would care at all. But it's Richie's promise as a player that animates them. Rosey pulls down a box of fifteen letters from college coaches inquiring about Richie Mount.

"If he gets as big as Rick, he'll be just as good as Rick," Rosey says. "Oh my, Rick just works that kid to death. Last summer I told him, 'Rick, it's hotter 'n hell outside,' but they just kept shootin'." Pete is chuckling. "I know. I called over there the other day. I think Rick answered. They were just a-pantin'. I said, 'What's goin' on?' You know them skip ropes with the metal in 'em? They were doin' a hundred of them at a time."

It's the stories, the shared opinions, the memories of four generations of common experience in Boone County sports that cements this friendship. The stories are pure pleasure to listen to, especially when they're about Rick, for his time was the brightest the sky ever got here.

"Fourth of July, when the carnival came around, they always had a basketball shoot," recalls Pete, his arm resting on a rack of basketballs. "Rick just wiped the whole thing out one night. He just kept a-hittin' 'em and won all the teddy bears." Rosey waits for him to finish. "Well what *happened* was, everyone was payin' Rick to shoot for them and then Rick was givin' 'em the bears."

Not long ago Rosey needed a little money for his summer program, so he put together the "Boone County All-Stars"— seniors from county high schools—and took them up to Clinton County to play their best. In the last fifteen seconds, Rosey stopped the game and sent Pete, Rick and Richie out together on the floor, along with Brian Walker and his dad. "I'll let you play," he told Pete, "but I don't want to see you runnin' up and down that floor." Of course, he couldn't stop Pete from getting in a shot.

It's a shame that Butch Neuman and John Mount couldn't have been there, too, and Doc Porter and the others from the great teams. The scene would have warmed the heart and maybe even the nose of Tom Dawson if he could have been looking in from his ladder.

Richie Mount began his freshman season starting on the Lebanon varsity, like his dad and grandpa. He scored twenty-two points in his first game, which Rick was too nervous to attend. Several games later, against still-hated Frankfort, many of whose fans wore red shirts in Richie's honor, he scored thirty-four points, hitting thirteen of his fifteen shots from the field. As everyone was quick to point out, Rick had never had a game that good as a freshman.

"Kids have it made now," says Rick. "It's a lot easier life. They've got their own cars. The dedication isn't as great as it was back when we played." Maybe so, but if Richie Mount's children go to Lebanon High, don't bet they'll spend their Friday nights bussing at the restaurants out by the cloverleaf. For three generations the Mounts have kept their values constant and their roots deep. Few American families have meant as much to one place for so long as the Mounts have to Lebanon, Indiana.

MEADOWOOD
PARK:
Banker's Paradise

Steve Woolsey remembers the beginning like this: "We were sittin' on basketballs, me and Alma, restin' between games, when a car pulled up way on the other side of the baseball diamond, over by where Scotty Neat lived. These two guys came walkin' through the woods like they were lost. It was the Van Arsdales. They looked so much alike it hurt your eyes. I literally thought I had been injured. A Van walks up to me and says, 'Is this Meadowood?' "

The Van Arsdale twins had just graduated from Indianapolis Manual High School, way on the other side of town from Speedway. They were relentlessly identical. After four years of high school, Dick had scored only a few more points than Tom. Dick was the valedictorian, Tom ranked third in the class. Their cheerleader girlfriends ranked second and sixth.

When it came time for the Indianapolis *Star* to name "Mr. Basketball" of 1961, the best player in the state, there was no choice but to crown them both. Likewise, after the state finals, the judges threw in the towel and gave them both Mental Attitude Awards. What fool was gonna stand up and say Tom had a better mental attitude than Dick?

After a while, people quit trying to tell them apart and treated them instead as proper nouns, e.g., "A Van was over at the Big Boy—I forget which one it was"—or "Lebanon Hardware had Carl Short, John McGlocklin and one of Vans—I forget which one it was." They were classic Jekyll and Hyde, true gentlemen off the court and pure mayhem on it. A Van didn't just pluck down a rebound, he tore it from the air, usually with both hands and splayed-out elbows.

They were the boys of that Hoosier summer, having just lost the state tournament in a heartbreaking overtime. "There's what *you* could be if you studied and practiced and turned that darned record player off," said everyone's parents. It got old. Besides, it was a lie. They were both 6'5" and there were two of them.

Woolsey must have thought he was hallucinating, for what he saw next was truly revolutionary. More cars skidded into the lot behind the Vans, and out of them spilled a dozen of the best black ball players in Indianapolis, the cream of Attucks and Tech and Shortridge.

Until that very moment in 1961, Speedway, Indiana, had been all but innocent of experience with nonwhites. Race relations in Speedway had mainly had to do with keeping cars off your lawn on Memorial Day. Speedway, as its residents are hair-trigger quick to point out, is the true home of the Indianapolis 500 race track, which lies *west* of the 16th Street bridge and therefore quite within the town's limits.

Speedway's four grade schools were named after the men who founded the track, namely, Carl G. Fisher, James A. Allison, Arthur C. Newby and Frank H. Wheeler. Fisher, among many other accomplishments, designed and developed Miami Beach. He also owned the first automobile in Indianapolis, and in 1907 he was fed up with the tire and engine failures that were plaguing the early luxury cars. What we need, he informed Allison, Newby and Wheeler

153

one evening at dinner, is a testing ground. He spread a napkin onto the table and took a pencil from his pocket. His companions leaned forward. Fisher drew an oval.

The track was finished in 1909, but Fisher wanted a town to go with it. Like the track, "Speedway City" was engineered, from the width of its streets to the form of its government, before land was purchased and lots sold. Its first streets were named after the autos of the day—Winton, Cord, Cole, Auburn and Ford. Two generations later, ranch-style, post–World War II homes sprang up along "drives" named Buick, Crosley, DeSoto, Nash and Lincoln.

The Speedway High School athletic teams were naturally called the Sparkplugs. Truancy increased in May as the drone of engines at the track, a mile away, beckoned to the boys through the school's open windows. When they were 15 or 16, their parents let them walk along 16th Street with their friends the night before the race. It was an important rite of passage, one that represented a powerful act of trust by the parents, for adult experiences were available in the flatbeds and trailers and vans that were backed up for miles behind the gates of the track.

At the time the Vans and their guests appeared at Meadowood, there were no black students in Speedway High School or black people living in Speedway, save for one family who sent their daughter to Shortridge at the start of junior high. Word that the Vans—and their extraordinary entourage—were in Meadowood Park roared through Speedway like a twin-engine Novi.

Playground basketball in Indianapolis has become something of a movable feast, and the Van Arsdales had a lot to do with that. Unlike most of America's major cities, there is no single court in Indianapolis where you can find the best competition. Rather, the best players telephone each other and agree on a court, driving in caravans to Warren Central for a week, Ben Davis for another and Meadowood for another.

Until they had a car of their own, the Vans were themselves driven around "Naptown" by an older teammate named Carl Short, into the inner-city black courts, looking for the best competition. Hallie Bryant, who grew up in a neighborhood into which few whites ventured, recalls the time the Vans showed up at his court, called the "Dust Bowl." "As twins, they must have felt very secure," says Bryant. "They were very brave and they played like football players. They were friendly, nice guys. Willie Gardner and I kind of broke 'em in here, and then we invited them back."

When the Vans got their licenses, they in turn took their new friends out of the city and into suburbs like Speedway. For about a month during the summer of 1961, the caravan appeared every evening at Meadowood Park, the Vans in the pace car, the blacks close behind. The crowds grew larger each night until Speedway residents encircled the court.

And then one night the Vans did not show up at Meadowood, and they never came back. But black players, properly introduced, have remained and the court has been integrated ever since. Meadowood Park remains one of the very few courts in Indianapolis where there is consistently good competition. At last count, twenty-one ABA or NBA players had played there.

Meadowood Park is a soft, delightful place to play, especially to those who grew up on hardscrabble courts. "It was surrounded by trees, and, you know, Indiana gets so humid in the summer," remembers George McGinnis, an NBA all-star forward who spent his adolescent summers there. "I had been used to playing in areas where, Jesus, if it got hot, that was it. Meadowood had that nice drinking fountain. The cement was nice and smooth, there were no cracks. The buckets were true, just the right height. But what I remember most is the competition. We had some hellacious games out there."

There were two adjacent full courts, but they were only about two-thirds as long as a regulation court, too short for cherry picking, as the habit of hanging around your own basket and not playing defense was called. The court was unlit, but in midsummer you could shoot by firefly until 9:30 or so. There were johns. In short, it was heaven.

In the summers, guys would start to show up about 6:00. The worse you were, the earlier you'd show, because the good players would come later, get picked and hold the court. Speedway High School players always tried to stay in at least until Morris Pollard, the Sparkplugs' coach, arrived. At the time, high school coaches in Indiana were not allowed to coach kids in the summer but could stand around the playgrounds and watch, the way ejected baseball managers remain in the shadows of clubhouse tunnels. On the last day of the season, Pollard would advise each of his returning players to "give me a good summer at Meadowood."

Two full-court games were played simultaneously. The game on the north court was the prestige game. If you lost that game and you were halfway decent, you would probably get picked by someone forming a south court game. This was an invitation to consider carefully. If you played on the south court you'd get laughed at on the way home, but at least you were playing. And to ditch your teammates in the middle of a south court game for a call to play on the north court was a serious breach of etiquette.

Sunday was big game day. Jim Price, who spent most of the '70s in NBA back courts, usually showed up with his brothers Mike—who played awhile with the Knicks—Jesse and Henry. The Price family could hold a court for a long time. "On a Sunday," says Jim Price, "my brothers and I wanted to play the whole day and never get beat. Only a couple of times did anyone stay in all day. I always liked to guard the person who had the name. It got my adrenaline flowin'. I hated for someone to score on me. It was pretty brutal out there. You could knock heads all day with someone and then leave the court together and go have a Dairy Queen."

Steve Woolsey—white, wide-hipped, not fast afoot and an indifferent defensive player—has probably scored more points at Meadowood than anyone else. There, he is best known as a banker. "Meadowood was Woolsey's home court," recalls George McGinnis. "No matter who came in there, Woolsey was gonna get his points, and he could hit them from thirty feet off that backboard. The backboards were perforated, full of little holes. You got the feeling that if he shot it too hard the ball would just stick there."

Construction of a new high school split Woolsey's neighborhood when he was a freshman, sending most of his junior high teammates on to Washington High, which won a state championship a few years later, and leaving him to bank them in for dreary teams at the new school. The disappointment lingers. " 'If' and 'but' are the two biggest words in the English language," he says. "But Washington, the '65 team, that was the greatest team in the last thirty-five years."

Meadowood became Woolsey's habitat, and he became, besides the master of its backboards, the court's historian and keenest observer of cultural trends. Woolsey recalls the dress code for whites of distinction during his salad days: "Let's start with the shoes. When I was young and we first went there—this was before the era of tube socks and leather shoes—we wore high-cut Chuck Taylor cons. We're talking about the early '60s.

"First leather shoes we ever saw, Rick Mount had 'em on, he had Adidas Super Stars. Some salesmen gave 'em to him to try 'em out, and naturally we thought he was nuts. We thought they looked like wrestling shoes. [Mount, remembering the incident, says they felt like bowling shoes. "I tried 'em one game, only got twenty-six points and never put 'em on again," he recalls.] He told us they were made out of kangaroo skin and came from New Zealand.

"We wore Wigwam socks, a wool sock that stayed up the best of any sock you could buy at the time. The T-shirt was the plain gray 'Russell Southern,' it's the one like coaches wear. No names. The trunks? West Point Pepperell."

That, at least, was the attire for fashion-conscious whites. Blacks could get away with anything. They'd show up walking cool and slow in shades and under wide brims, wearing bright-colored, floppy shirts or clingy tank tops. Often they wore several layers of sweat clothes, which they made a point of peeling off very slowly, as if they expected to hold the north court for a week or so and didn't want to peak early.

Sometimes they just wore street clothes. "The greatest humiliation at Meadowood was getting beat by people wearing street shoes," says Woolsey. "I remember one time we were playing over there and these four guys came over wearing trench coats. They had been to a picnic in the park and one of them was wearing wing tips, one guy had Hush Puppies and another had on penny loafers. We were playing four-on-four, me and Keller and Alma and someone, and they beat us. I said, 'We'll take you again,' and they beat us again."

Unlike the playground rules elsewhere, which adapt freely to local circumstances, Indiana playground rules seek always to imitate real game conditions. Indiana is, for example, a last bastion of "loser's outs." This means that in Hoosierland, when your team scores a basket, the other team gets the ball, just as in a real game. Most other places it's "make it/take it," meaning if you score, you keep the ball.

Indiana playground rules encourage outside shooting, even in the hearts of the state's biggest cities. In Indiana the ball is always taken back behind the free-throw line to start a new play. In some other places, like New York, kids play "straight up," meaning a missed shot can be tapped back in by either team. This has the effect of compressing the area of play, breeding great rebounders but poor shooters.

In Indiana, you choose up sides and settle disputes by "shooting for it" (it is said, "the ball never lies"), and you keep score by twos, just as in a real game. A Hoosier and a Brooklynite may play a game to eleven baskets, but if they play in Indiana, the winner will have twenty-two points and, in Brooklyn, eleven.

The differences are jarring when Hoosiers first play outside of Indiana. "When I played in the service," says Woolsey, "it was like learning a foreign language. We played by ones and my mind was still converting to twos. It's like kilometers to miles. I'd get in the middle of a game and I couldn't think of where I was at."

When dusk would gather over the court, the black players would drive on back to the city, once again leaving the court to the white kids who lived nearby. They shot in the dark, navigating by the sound of the ball against the rim and the net, talking mainly about girls or the best games of the night.

Sometimes the conversation would drift into the differences between blacks and whites. There was constant speculation about why blacks did so well at basketball. The prevailing view was that they enjoyed some physiological advantage. There was no denying that almost any black could outjump almost any white at Meadowood.

The notion that black kids cared more and played more because basketball was the road out of the ghetto was widely debunked. How could anyone care more or play more than they did? You couldn't play more than every day. On the other hand, it was true that almost all the Speedway kids, at least, were bound for some college. That was taken as a birthright. Maybe that made basketball mean a little less.

Blacks learned as much about whites at Meadowood as whites about blacks. George McGinnis grew up in a poor area on Indianapolis' west side. As an adult, George played for Indiana, Denver and Philadelphia as a 6'8", 235-pound forward. Even as an adolescent, he'd been big and heavily muscled.

He was not sure Speedway would welcome him with open arms. He remembers his first trip to the park very well. "I first came out to Meadowood in my eighth-grade

Before black basketball players appeared at Meadowood Park, race relations in Speedway, Indiana, had meant keeping cars off your lawn during Memorial Day weekend. *(Phillip M. Hoose)*

God made Meadowwood's soft, perforated backboards for bank shot artists. *(Phillip M. Hoose)*

Three ex-Speedway High Sparkplugs on a Sunday afternoon at Meadowood Park. *(Phillip M. Hoose)*

year. I can't remember who drove me out. I drove past Speedway High School with its swimming pool and that big parking lot and past the nice houses and well-kept lawns, and I thought, "What am I doing here?"

But McGinnis, who has an open and adventuresome personality, found friends in Speedway. When he got really thirsty, he walked over to Fuzzy Jordan's house and asked if he could drink out of the spigot. Often as not, Fuzzy's wife, Marge, would bring out a pitcher of ice water.

"I remember a really nice kid, Tom Gilbert," says George. "He played for Speedway High and his family lived by the Meadowood court. I'd play so hard and get real hungry and I'd go home with Tom and say, 'Mrs. Gilbert, can I have a baloney sandwich or something?' and his mother would fix me one.

"His mom and dad were so nice to me. They had a little place on a lake, and the Gilberts would take me down there and let me stay the weekend. They got me into water skiing. My dad worked two jobs and really didn't have time to teach me to drive. Mr. Gilbert taught me how to drive down at the lake in his three-speed jeep."

Both blacks and whites seem proud of the court's tradition of racial harmony. Most fights of all kinds are broken up quickly. But the games are rough, and the suburban setting produces a background tension that has from time to time erupted into violence. Steve Woolsey's skull was fractured once in an interracial brawl that escalated from a casual remark. That evening, Woolsey regained consciousness in a hospital bed, looking up at the minister of his church. "I thought I was ready to bite the dust," he recalls, "but it turned out my minister was there visiting an old lady upstairs when he happened to run into my dad and then came down to see me. The other thing I couldn't figure out was why I was dying with my jock on."

If Meadowood had a true king, it was a white kid named Bill Keller. He started showing up at the park as a chubby seventh-grader, always in the company of five or six older kids. His escorts—they were more like chaperones—seemed to enjoy watching young Billy burn tread marks into those who underestimated him.

Keller had started playing as a posttoddler, tagging along behind his brother Bernie, seven years his senior. He couldn't see why they didn't want him. "Bernie's friends used to call me 'tubby' and 'meatballs,' " he says, still a little miffed. "He'd take me over to School 67 to play and ride my bike home and make me run behind him. They would usually let me in their games when they were tired and it was dark and you could barely see the rim. I was always too young or too short . . . you develop a real sense of pride when people won't let you do something."

As Keller outgrew his baby fat, he began to develop a big reputation, both at Washington High School and at Meadowood. He was quick, strong and a great shooter. Above all, he had a death-before-dishonor approach to losing. Jim Price remembers guarding Keller at Meadowood very clearly: "I think I was a freshman when he was a junior, but he already had a big name. It was like playin' against a rock. He never backed down. He outhustled you. When the smoke cleared, he was ahead."

The Kellers lived one block away from the Speedway town limits, maybe a hundred feet east of the 16th Street bridge. The town would gladly have paid to move their house that one block, especially in Bill's senior year, when he led Washington High to the state championship and was named "Mr. Basketball."

Like Bernie's friends, most of America's major colleges thought Keller, who stopped growing at 5'10", was too little to play. The Citadel, a military school in Virginia, was one of the few colleges that really went after him. They flew him down for a visit, and the guys at Meadowood waited breathlessly for a trip report, hoping he had been offered a car or some money. Instead, he came back with several packages of Fruit of the Loom underwear, courtesy of an alum associated with the firm.

Keller went to Purdue, where he played for an NCAA runner-up team, and in his senior year he was named America's best player under six feet tall. In the summers, he used to bring his Purdue teammates back to Meadowood for some real competition. One summer evening, he brought future Portland Trailblazer Herman Gilliam with him. They happened to walk onto the court during a between-games dunking contest.

Now this was not the NBA. The typical Meadowood contestant, rather than trying to decide between a helicopter jam or a 360, was standing in line, licking his fingers and trying to get the ball to stick in his palm, wishing he had bigger hands and thinking about getting his steps right. The most common results were either that the ball would slip out of the leaper's hand on the way up or slam into the back of the rim and out into the woods.

Gilliam, a slim 6'2½", took his place at the end of the line, unrecognized in shades and a big straw hat. When his turn came, he picked up a second ball, took three giant strides, soared into the air and slammed both balls, *wham bam*, through the hoop and onto the cement. Woolsey rates it as the most exciting moment in Meadowood's history. "The brothers went crazy. A guy named Al Fox ran through the park, just yelling, "Two at a time, two at a time.""

Bill Keller pushes away a bowl of chips. "You know what I really miss?" he says. "The money has been pretty good, the opportunities were good, but I miss the conditioning. I watch the pros on TV, and I think, 'I used to be in that good of shape.' It would take a lot of work to get back."

Keller is mulling this over in the sunken living room of a lovely split-level home "right next to Bob MacIntyre of Bob MacIntyre Chevy" in a community north of Indianapolis. He is the only male in a cheerful, sports-oriented family of four.

Keller's wife, Joyce, is opening mail orders for "Billy Keller's All-Star Summer Basketball Camp." When things get too quiet, Jeannie, his elder stepdaughter, slips down to the trophy room and puts "The Ballad of Billy Keller," a song which sold quite well in Indiana several years ago, on the stereo console Keller won as the Most Popular Indiana Pacer. He won the award so many times the club discontinued it for a while. Hearing the song, Joyce shrieks in what is probably mock agony.

After a nine-year career as a high-scoring guard with the Pacers, a knee injury cut short Keller's career one year before the ABA merged with the NBA. All those years he'd continued his struggle to prove he was big enough to play basketball.

Ironically, he was adored throughout Hoosierland in large part because he was short. Watching Billy Keller zip through the giraffes and greyhounds, firing up three-pointers on the dead run and scooping the ball over their giant limbs and into the net, it was easy for the thousands of ex–high school players to believe that if they had just stayed in shape and wanted it a little more, they could have been out there. Had he been 6'4" and 200 pounds, Bill Keller might have been an all-pro. At 5'10" and 185, he was a friend.

George McGinnis, who last played in the NBA in 1982, now lives with his wife, Linda, and son, Tony, in a very large mock-Tudor home in Denver. Cedars flank the front steps and fan out to a privacy fence not quite tall enough to conceal a basketball goal. "How many rooms do we have here?" he repeats. "Oh, God, I don't know. I never counted." He says he has invested his basketball earnings well, and that for a kid from Haughville, as his neighborhood was called, he's done all right.

"You know, when I first started playing my dad was totally against it," George says, "because he thought I should be working. He used to scream at my mother for buying me tennis shoes. But then I got better and better and we won the state championship and in my senior year he was all gung-ho."

The last game McGinnis' father saw him play, just before he died in a construction accident, was a high school all-star game between Indiana and Kentucky in which McGinnis scored fifty-three points and took down thirty rebounds. It was the greatest performance in the history of the half-century-old interstate series, on which much Hoosier ego rests.

"Maybe God just had it that way," says McGinnis, "because it was probably the best game of my life. He was hugging me on the way back in the car and I can still remember him saying, 'You're going to be a *pro*, and do you know what I want when you get that first big piece of money? I don't want a car, no way, what I want is a *helicopter*.' "

After briefly dominating the Big Ten at Indiana University McGinnis became an all-star as a professional player. Then, after three fine seasons with the Philadelphia '76ers, he was traded to Denver. A proud and sensitive man, he was bitterly hurt, and the experience sent him into a tailspin. "It was the first time I was ever rejected," he says. "I started questioning, questioning, questioning," he says, eyes closed. "I never really was the same."

"In pro sports," he says, "I never really felt the *glue* I felt at IU or in high school. About the minute you got to know a guy, within a week he was gone and they bring in another guy the next day like nothing ever happened. It was hard for me to accept that."

His mood lightening, McGinnis takes a basketball down from the mantelpiece. "When I was in eighth grade, Billy Keller showed me this drill, and to this day I show it to kids and they can't do it. See, you take the ball right here between your legs, you drop it, catch it with the left hand, go around this leg, drop it and catch it with your right hand." The ball is a blur between McGinnis' legs. The percussion echoes in the marble of his living room. Beads of sweat appear on his brow.

"You know," he says, "coming from where I did, I thought all the people in Speedway were millionaires, and I thought most people were unapproachable because of that. They were just basically hard-working middle class, but I don't think we were able to understand that. To us, middle class was like rich. I thought wealth separated people, and I've learned a lot differently since then. People at Meadowood were nice and receptive to me, and I've never forgotten that."

Steve Woolsey now lives in a three-bedroom ranch house in a small town north of Indianapolis with his wife, Jeannie, their 17-year-old daughter, Lori, and their 5-year-old son, Scott. He drives a feeder truck for United Parcel, the job he has held ever since he came home from a brief stint at a junior college in Wyoming. "I could have done just about anything I wanted to," Woolsey says, "but here I am out driving a truck. I make more money than any high school coach in Indiana, but money doesn't necessarily mean success."

He has come to regard his boyhood obsession with basketball as a poor investment. "I played five, six, seven hours a day, knew every statistic, read every book, knew every ball player that ever played. I dreamed about basketball at night. It never occurred to me that I would have to work for a living."

Still, old habits are hard to break. On summer Sunday afternoons, Steve drives Jeannie into Speedway, drops her off at the Speedway Shopping Center and heads for the park. Now 39, balding and slower than ever, he still knows the perforated backboards as no one else ever has. "There is just something about that design, the aluminum-and-steel backboards. They just . . . *boom* . . . you can just hear it."

Steve is recounting the experience of watching Scotty enter the world. "Yeah, the miracle of life," says Steve, "you can't put the feeling of seeing your child born into words." Up to now, Jeannie has been listening quietly. "Do you know what I said to Steve when he saw Scotty on the delivery table?" she asks. "I said, 'Now you have someone to take to Meadowood.' "

It's late, and Bill Keller's thoughts are drifting. "When it got dark out there, it really got dark with all those trees. There was one light by the parking lot and you could kind of see the light coming through the trees. You could just hear your voices and the balls bouncing and the nets when you hit.

"Sometimes when we're on that side of town, I've taken Joyce by Meadowood, just driving by. I try to explain to her what the place is all about. We park in the parking lot out there and watch the guys playing, just sit back and watch. Nobody knows I'm there, and I think about all that went on there. Then she'll say, 'Have you seen enough?' and I start the car, but I always take the longest way around so I'll catch a glimpse of Meadowood from all angles."

7

STEVE ALFORD:

Megahero

"**I** remember sitting on a bench with my father when he was a high school coach at Monroe County when I was three and since then I can't remember a day in my life that I haven't picked up a basketball."
—STEVE ALFORD, 1984

"I've got the most unusual Steve Alford story that you've ever heard," says Norm Held, coach of the Anderson Indians. "We had a game here in the Wigwam against New Castle. We're one point ahead with five seconds to play, and Alford gets fouled. He has two shots. We call time out to let him think about the first one. We really weren't letting him think about it 'cause you know he's gonna make it. Actually, we were worrying about how to score when we got the ball again.

"So we go back out there and he *missed* the first one. So we called another time out. We were thinking about the overtime. We went out again and he missed *another* one. He probably can't remember a game in his life when he missed two free throws in a row. Mike Chappel, who writes for the newspaper, had the best line the next morning. He wrote, 'Well, I'da lost my farm, how about you?' "

Shaking his head, Steve Alford confirms the story. "That's the only time I've ever missed two in a row in a game. The first one hit the back of the rim and the second one was in and out. I don't know what happened. . . . At first I was shocked, and then I got very upset. I told Coach I was going to stay in the gym all night and shoot free throws."

Steve Alford is known to basketball fans throughout America as the star of Bobby Knight's Indiana University basketball team and throughout the world as the youngest member of the 1984 U.S. Olympic basketball team. But he became an immortal in Indiana as a high school player.

In his senior year, Steve averaged over thirty-seven points per game and was named the outstanding player in the state. Always double- and triple-teamed, he hit over 60 percent of his field goals and 94.4 percent of his free throws. In that year he was the best free-throw shooter on earth, high school, college or pro.

For connoisseurs, *the* Steve Alford game came in the semistate round of the state tourney in his senior year. Against a rugged team from Indianapolis Broad Ripple, Steve drove again and again toward the hoop, stopped, spun away and faked his jump shot. Bodies rocketed into the air, ready to slam the ball into his tonsils. As the first defenders came down upon him he floated shot after shot through the hoop, got up and walked to the free-throw line.

He shot twenty-five free throws that game. They all went in. Only one even nicked the rim in passing through. When all was done, he had scored fifty-seven points, the most ever in an Indiana tournament game. At the beginning of the game, people were talking "Mr. Basketball," in itself a form of sainthood. When they flicked their sets off, he was sitting at the head table, dining with the likes of Oscar, McGinnis, Mount and Bird.

As he describes his elder son's early childhood, a tone of wonderment is present in Sam Alford's voice. "He started sitting on the bench with me when he was 3. From then until he graduated from high school, he only missed two of my games—one to go to a free-throw shooting contest in Kansas City with his mother and once when he had chicken pox."

Sam Alford, 42, the head coach of the New Castle Trojans, has been coaching high school players in Indiana more than half his lifetime. Here in the Vienna of basketball, it is easy to imagine him as the father of a musical prodigy, describing perhaps the first time he heard a scale creep from his infant son's fingers on the drawing room piano.

"He learned to count by watching the scoreboards," Sam says. "He used to sit on the bench with me, holding a clipboard and a piece of paper. Every time the scoreboard would change he'd draw a line through the old numbers and write down the new ones."

And it was never hard to shop for Steve. "He never asked us for a gun or a holster. He never wanted to play cowboys. He always used to throw blocks at Tinkertoy cans and shoot Ping-Pong balls at bowls and glasses. I never had to force basketball on him," says Sam, almost apologetically.

Unlike the urban players whose game evolves in Darwinian playground competition, Steve Alford developed his skills in isolation. The New Castle gym was his monastery. He purged his game of imperfections each day in exacting private sessions that lasted long after regular basketball practice. A missed free throw warranted an act of mortification, namely twenty-five fingertip pushups. Each summer when the Alfords went to Florida for a week or two, the basketball went along. They looked for motels with basketball courts.

"He punished himself," says Sam Alford. "On the court in our driveway other kids would come in for a bottle of pop between games. Steve would rest by shooting free throws." When they heard the ball thumping at midnight, the Alfords knew Steve couldn't sleep.

He allowed no one to interrupt his private sessions. "When I am working out individually, I don't want a girlfriend, I don't want a mom, I don't want a dad, I don't want anybody to bother me, and if they do I get very nasty and upset with them because I find my time in the gym is to do what I want. Each new day I wanted to do it right after I woke up," he says. "It was so fun I wanted to do it over and over again.

"I competed within my own body, within my own mind . . . it wasn't until high school that I wanted to play against good competition. I did all kinds of imaginary things. I'd line up twenty chairs on one end of the court and work on my dribbling. I'd dribble between each chair, one behind my back, one between my legs, spin move right, spin move left, then I would put the chairs in a circle and put a ball on each chair and I'd have to hit two shots with each chair before I could move on to the next.

"I'd set up a chair and put a broom in it, shoot over a broom, just like it would be a hand in my face. I dreamed that the brooms were Oscar Robertson or Jerry West, and I was playing against the Bucks or Lakers."

The real Oscar Robertson, the one whose strong hands swatted NBA defenders away as if they were clouds of gnats, prefers education by fire. "Shooting and dribbling, you can do a lot of that alone," Robertson says, "but I think the most improvement comes when you get into competition, in the battle. Because no matter what happens, you know that chair does not have a hand and a person may not move the way you planned. Basketball is reaction to different situations. You have to react to what happens to you . . . after a while it becomes automatic."

Told of Oscar's opinion, Alford replied, "Oscar had some ability that I didn't have and I think he could go out in alley ball and do those sorts of things. I had to become a great shooter. I agree with the pressure bit, but now that I've developed the shot I have, it doesn't matter who is up in my face. Pressure doesn't bother me, because I've worked that out on my own."

At 19, Steve Alford comes across as an obliging and unusually controlled young man. He is 6′2″ and slender— about 160 pounds—with a well-proportioned upper body; he looks like a rather tall gymnast. He is an ad for clean living and good grooming. His hair, carefully layered and parted in the center, lies perfectly. Compared to Steve Alford, Steve Garvey looks like a Rastafarian.

He has long been used to being interviewed. Answers to questions can sometimes seem a little canned, with more "cherished moments" and "youngsters" than you would expect in the typical 19-year-old's vocabulary.

But then Steve Alford, like every member of Sam Alford's New Castle Trojans basketball teams, has been groomed for life as a public figure, for a basketball player in New Castle represents the town. "Our players can't have beards or moustaches, hair is kept off the ears," says Sam. "When we go on the road, we wear sport coats or sweaters with ties. When we eat, the seniors go first. We won't let our players wear earrings;"—there is something unsettling about the image of Steve Alford with pierced ears—"we try to be very polite with everything we do. We want every young boy growing up in New Castle to say to himself, I want to be a Trojan when I grow up."

As a basketball hero from a basketball town in a basketball state, Steve Alford has come to represent idealized Indiana. While Steve is not yet as official a symbol as Larry Bird or Bobby Knight—their faces would not seem out of place on a stamp or coin in Hoosierland—he may come closer to the way many Hoosiers would like to think of themselves.

Steve is forced to manage his time carefully, for the demands are incessant, from celebrity golf tournaments to television talk shows to requests for autographs, which he signs "Yours in Christ." He prays before and after each game. "I talk to God whenever I get the chance," Steve has said. "It's like when I dedicate myself to basketball, I do the same to Him, because He has given me all that I have today."

Very occasionally, the 19-year-old boy pops out for a moment, like a hair that won't lie down. As Sam tells the story of the adolescent Steve hiding in the closet with a tape recorder, imitating a baseball announcer's play-by-play style, Steve scrunches up in his chair and begins to giggle. The giggle turns to laughter, and soon he is blushing furiously. At another point, Sam mistakenly calls Steve by his younger brother's name. When the interview is finished, Steve walks to his father's side. "Dad," he says softly, "you called me Sean again."

Both Sam and Steve admire Sean Alford, two years younger than Steve, for his adjustment to Steve's celebrity. "He'll answer the door and people'll walk right past him, looking

Mr. Basketball, Steve Alford: sainthood, Hoosier-style.
(Frank H. Fisse)

Steve Alford drives for two of his fifty-seven points
against Indianapolis Broad Ripple, the game that qualified Steve's face for a Hoosier Mt. Rushmore, should one
ever erupt through an Indiana cornfield. *(Frank H. Fisse)*
(RIGHT)

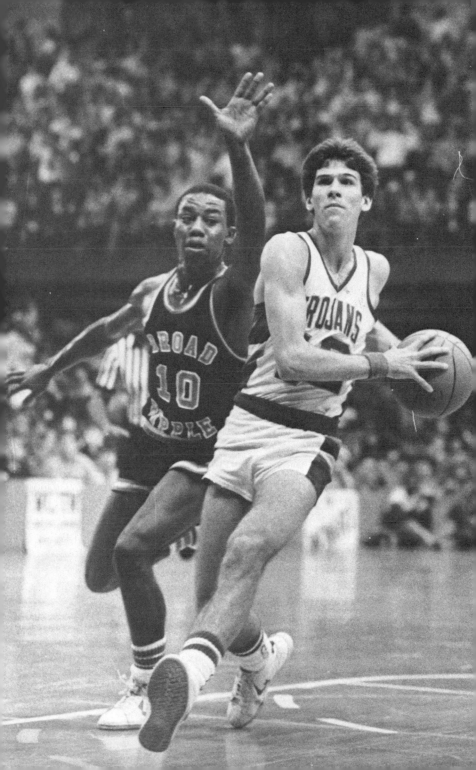

for Steve," says Sam. "This past year, he's had the toughest
job in the U.S."

"When we came here I was 9 years old, and Dad
thought it would be tough to get me to move from Martinsville," Steve says. "But when New Castle offered him
a job and I first saw this place there was no question this
is where I wanted to be."

Steve is speaking from the bottom row of bleachers in
what a banner stretched across one wall proclaims to be
"The largest and finest high school field house in the world."
The basketball floor is set in the bottom of a giant crater
whose 9,325 seats (New Castle High's enrollment is 1,150)
begin in a wide circle at street level. From courtside, students jogging around the track at the top look like mules
working their way slowly around the south rim. To visiting
teams, this must seem like the pit of Hell.

"My junior year we played Cincinnati Moeller here,"
says Steve, referring to a high school best known for its
nationally ranked football teams. They walked into the field
house on Saturday morning, while we were practicing. They
were huge, 6'6", 6'7", all football players. I remember looking up and you could just see them thinking, 'Oh my God,
what *is* this place?'

"They took the floor that night, and Dad said, 'Okay,
they've never played here before and the place is a sellout,
so let's pick 'em up full court right from the start.' The first
twelve trips down the court they didn't get past midcourt
line. At one time it was 20 to 0."

Old-timers in New Castle say the gym was needed to
break the "Muncie syndrome," a spell alleged to have beset
the New Castle Trojans when they played the regional

tourney in the Muncie gym. There was the time the lights went off in the middle of a shot and the buzzer went off in the middle of a rally—or did the lights go off in the middle of the shot?—oh, whatever, there was a half-century's worth of bad calls.

So the Monday Morning Club, as the civic leaders that meet for coffee at Kresge's every Monday morning are known, decided to build a gym big enough to host their own regional. Consequently, almost everyone in New Castle can find a "Gym Now" bond in an old scrapbook. When the dust cleared in 1959 the world's champion high school gym stood in a town of 19,500.

Steve Alford squints up at the joggers. "The first thing I told myself, ten years ago," he says, "was that I wanted to fill this place. My junior and senior years we filled it pretty regularly."

"You expect me to remember a third grader?" says Bobby Knight, glancing sideways at the clown who had asked him to recall his first impression of Steve Alford. Steve, while more indulgent, is equally vague about their first meeting. "It was such a long time ago," says Steve. "I went to his basketball camp nine straight summers."

Knight's courtship of Steve was brief and to the point. First he tested the air for rivals; he thought he caught wind of Purdue. "He was teasing me," recalls Steve. "Dad had a player named Jerry Sichting and Jerry ended up going to Purdue. Jerry was sort of a hero of mine. So whenever I went to camp Coach Knight would ask me if my dad had convinced me to be a Boilermaker fan yet. I told him, 'Well, I'm sure a Jerry Sichting fan.' Coach says now he made a mistake in not recruiting Jerry."

Then he proposed. "At the end of my sophomore year, late in the summer, I went down there [to Bloomington]. He just said, 'If you're interested in coming here, we're interested in having you, so let's make a verbal commitment now and forget about the recruiting.' "

And the marriage. "You don't actually realize what it's going to be like until you go through it," said Steve after his freshman year. "It's something I'll be able to cherish, and hopefully someday I'll be able to write a book about my four years at Indiana. There'll be some great times and there are going to be some bad times when things don't go as well. I think the bad times are probably better learning experiences than the good times."

Steve's freshman season could surely be likened to a honeymoon. Defenders behaved like broomsticks as Steve broke ancient shooting records at Indiana University. In the NCAA tourney, he gave an inspiring performance in a nationally televised upset of top-ranked North Carolina. In the game's closing minutes he was treating the likes of Michael Jordan and Sam Perkins as if they were Broad Ripple High again, drawing fouls and swishing free throws. At the end of his storybook season, coach Knight selected Steve as the youngest member of the U.S. Olympic basketball team. Steve played impressively and his team won an easy gold medal.

As his sophomore season began, he was a member of most of the preseason All-America teams, ranked as one of the best two or three guards in America. He started strongly, but then he encountered a major learning experience. The baskets seemed to have shrunk. During one six-game stretch, Steve shot 26 percent from the field. Indiana quickly fell out of the Big Ten race.

He was exhausted, having played competitive basketball

for nearly three years without a break. His legs felt like lead. Because Indiana's forwards were not scoring threats, teams ganged up on Steve and center Uwe Blab. After holding Steve to seven points, Illinois guard Doug Altenberger, 6'4" and 200 pounds, explained the secret of his success: "I made sure everywhere he went he got bumped and that when he got open he was too tired to shoot it."

"There are some things he can't do," Knight told the Indianapolis *News* during Steve's slump. "When you've got a kid like Steve who is not quick, then taking the shot away from him is really going to affect the way he plays . . . we've got to do some things better in other ways than we have with Alford."

"I'd like to settle down and play pro ball," Steve Alford says. "It's a longer season and I like playing basketball as long as possible. I've worked so hard and worked so long. It seems like I've been playing forever. I'd like to start getting paid for playing."

But Steve is smart enough to know that NBA basketball is a different game, a realm where even the best shooters tend to be tall, broad and tough. "I know there's a chance that I might not even get to play pro ball," Steve says. "But nobody else knows how hard I've worked; only I know that. I like people to say, 'He's not good enough, he doesn't know what he's getting into.' When I left high school, everyone said I was too skinny, too light, that I couldn't take the Big Ten season. But [in his freshman year] I was third in the league in scoring and I did most of the bruising. I hope that by the time I'm a senior, my stock is really going to be good."

According to Marty Blake, director of scouting for the

NBA, he'll indeed have to wait till then to know the value of his stock. "He's gonna have to get stronger, although Jerry West only weighed about 170. He's got speed and quickness, he's a very smart basketball player and he can get his shot. He has good range. I don't know if he's gonna be a *great* player, but he has the tools. He did a terrific job on the Olympic team."

Blake agrees with Bobby Knight that having made the Olympic team put unnecessary pressure on Steve as a sophomore. Knight has said that picking Steve did not mean that Steve was necessarily one of the best dozen players in the United States. He needed a shooter, and Alford was the best shooter in camp, no more, no less.

And after the NBA? "I don't want to leave basketball, I can't leave basketball. I want to do it as long as I possibly can. I'd like to coach at the college level. I would only coach high school in the state of Indiana."

And romance? "Basketball is number one to me and nothing is going to interfere with that," Steve says. "I had a date for the prom but I found out that I was invited to go to the Dapper Dan [a high school all-star game] in Pennsylvania the same night and I went to the tournament. The girl took it well, she's in athletics so she understood. But if I have a girl, she has to be understanding."

Asked if he feels Steve missed anything of childhood by devoting so much of it to a single pursuit, Sam Alford replies quickly, "I certainly do, but I don't think he knows that. Maybe when he has children of his own he'll realize what he has missed.

"I think a lot will depend on the next few years for

him. Up to this time basketball has been the number-one thing in his life, but he'll learn that each year from now on it will become tougher and more of a job. If he can keep it fun, keep in the right perspective, that would be good."

JUDI WARREN AND THE WARSAW TIGERS:

Moving

into

the Front Court

Patricia Roy's office walls are
covered with glossy photos of a high school girl with her
hair in a bowl cut, the way boys wear it in Maine, only
with the ends turned neatly under. She is steering what
seems to be a huge basketball around and through much
bigger girls. Her body seems almost horizontal to the court,
she is driving so hard.

Commissioner Roy is in charge of all girls' sports programs for the Indiana High School Athletic Association.
She pushed hard for a girls' basketball tournament, and its
success, whose magnitude not even she could have imag-
ined, is due in large part to the girl whose image fills her
walls.

"I thank God for Judi Warren," Roy says of the girl.
"She's our Billie Jean King. She's the spark that ignited
girls' basketball in Indiana. It was scary to start out in what
had been a boys' program, but she was a little kid with a
lot of fire. She caught people's imaginations. We were lucky
she started when she did."

Girls' basketball has become a major force in Indiana.
Girls have forced their brothers to share the driveways and
the boys' coaches to share the keys to the high school gym.
Their knees are braced, their hair is pulled back from their
eyes and their ankles are taped. Their mothers no longer
wash their sweaty uniforms—they get tossed in the team's

laundry bin. Many girls will not waste time or risk injury—and the loss of a scholarship—by playing other sports.

In 1984 the Indiana Girls' State Championship game drew over 15,000 fans, the largest crowd ever to watch a girls' five-player high school basketball game in the United States (there have been larger crowds in Iowa, where girls play six to a side). The TV ratings were impressive.

It wasn't always this way. Girls first played basketball in Indiana in 1898, wearing bloomers, middy blouses and high cotton stockings. Sponsors helped the girls withstand the mighty temptation to roll the stockings down—thus exposing the knees—when they got hot and itchy during a game.

Since competition produced excitement and sweat, men were not allowed to watch the games in many towns. The exertion required to play basketball was believed to be quite dangerous, especially when the "curse" came around. "It must always be remembered that the fascination of the game is so great . . . that there is temptation to play at the time of menstruation," wrote Dr. J. Anna Norris. "It is accepted by most authorities that there should be no basketball during at least three days at that time."

For most of a century, the game was a form of tranquil exercises staged in a largely social setting. "Better than winning honor in basketball is deserving credit for lady-like conduct, not only in the game but before and after," wrote the Hobart, Indiana, *Gazette* in 1915.

Little girls who played ball were called tomboys. Those who persisted into high school entered rougher waters. *They* became known as "jocks," and it was assumed that boys who dated them did so because they couldn't get anyone else. Some women coaches who spent a lot of time with their players were called "dykes," and more than a few were driven from Indiana schools like witches in Salem.

When Judi Warren and her Warsaw High teammates first started, there were no female role models, few resources and little encouragement. But they didn't care, at least not at first. Like thousands of Hoosier kids, they were in love with the game. To them, it was just a ball and a hoop.

"Enthusiasm without hysteria" was the goal of Miss Senda Berenson, who introduced Dr. Naismith's game to America's colleges in 1893. Applied to basketball in Indiana, that is a contradiction in terms. One dramatic winter night in 1976, the Warsaw tigers proved that "Hoosier Hysteria" is gender-free.

Judi Warren had a problem: the Lions Club had chosen her "Miss Claypool," queen of the fair, and there was no way out of it. She didn't want to be "Miss Claypool," she didn't *feel* like "Miss Claypool," but there she was, and they had to do something with her hair.

This required a team meeting. Cindy Ross, the team's center and cocaptain, went with her to a beautician, for this was not a job for a barber. Before, Judi had just gone to the barber with her dad on a Saturday morning and had her hair cut straight. She wanted it simple, for she had no time to bother with curlers.

Janet Warren had long ago given up on making a homemaker of her younger daughter. Judi wouldn't come in for piano lessons, dropped band, and seemed to drift away from housework. At least Janet *had* put her foot down on 4-H. A girl should be able to cook and sew, and besides, Janet Warren was the Claypool 4-H leader and her own daughter was going to be there.

Not that Janet hadn't liked sports herself. She had played

a little basketball at Claypool High, six girls on a team. Then again, she had done everything else, too: led cheers, blown horns in the band, hammed it up in the school plays. "The class just wouldn't have functioned if I hadn't have been there," she says. Certainly, her thirteen classmates would have noticed her absence.

But all Judi had ever seemed to want to do was play ball. As a little girl, when she got mad or moody, after dinner or before dinner, she'd take a ball out to the driveway and practice throwing it against the chimney and catching it. Then she started throwing it into the basket. Then, when her elder brother Jack's friends came over, she'd play with them. Even though she was six years younger and a girl, they all seemed to love her, partly because she'd chase the ball for them all day long. It worried Janet that Judi wasn't meeting any girls. It was good that she was dedicated to something, but this didn't seem, well, *rounded*.

Despite her misgivings, Janet Warren was above all a devoted and supportive mother. She made time to see Judi's games and arranged meals around practice. As a Hoosier, and having herself married Layne Warren, a pretty slick guard from Claypool, she had seen enough basketball to know that Judi was good. Judi was smaller than everyone else, but she seemed to get up and down the court twice as fast as the other girls. She had always been exceptionally well-coordinated. There had been no training wheels on Judi's bike; one day she'd just pedaled off to kindergarten.

While Judi was in grade school, all the Kosciusko County schools, Claypool and Atwood and Leesburg and Silver Lake, were consolidated into Warsaw High School, absorbed like provinces into a central soviet. "Our towns disintegrated," Janet said. "The towns became shambles of communities. When you take the teenagers out of a community there's not much left." Condemned to go to high school in a faceless institution, Judi amazed her mother by remarking one night at dinner that she was happy to be going to a school that had a sports program for girls. It was hard to figure her out.

And when the time came, just as her mother had predicted, Judi found Warsaw High to be a lot different from Claypool. It was so big that Judi told her she couldn't find the john until the third day. To Janet's relief, she did find girlfriends, though, although there was a catch. These girls were as nuts about sports as Judi.

Actually, Lisa Vandermark, Cindy Ross and Cathy Folk had known about Judi Warren for a long time, for Judi's Claypool grade school teams kept beating theirs. Actually, Judi had met Cindy by falling on her in a sixth-grade basketball game. Judi swears Cindy tripped her.

Cindy was a head taller than Judi, with long blond hair. All through grade school, Cindy had worn shorts underneath her skirts, so she could whip off the skirt and play tag and dodge ball with the boys at recess.

The Rosses lived in town. Cindy's parents encouraged her desire to be an athlete. Bill Ross was a cheerful and muscular man who followed sports but who had himself started working too early in life to try out for the high school teams. He told his daughter that the main thing was to love something, learn to do it well and not to quit when the going got tough.

The whole family played twenty-one and shot free throws in the driveway, mom spinning 'em up underhanded and dad overhanded and the three younger brothers heaving them up any way they could. On the day Cindy announced that she had entered the local AAU track meet as a javelin thrower, they were delighted. All six piled into the car and drove to the park for a Sunday afternoon of javelin throwing. It didn't matter at all that no one had a clue how to throw a javelin.

Judi, Cindy, Lisa and Cathy ran track and played badminton in the fall, tennis in the spring and basketball in the winter. They spent all their free time together. Their parents began to get to know one another, too, as the girls stayed at each others' homes on weekends.

They spent their winter Saturday afternoons like boys throughout Indiana, watching and listening to basketball games, munching chips and tugging on sodas. If they didn't like the announcer on TV, they turned the sound down and listened to a second game on the radio.

At halftime they ran outside and practiced new plays, or, if it was too cold, they played euchre. UCLA was their favorite team, because the Bruins ran and pressed and played the whole court, just as their junior high coach, Vivian Eigemiller, had taught them to do. They worked on the timing of their own low-altitude version of the alley-oop pass, with Judi as Greg Lee and Cindy as Bill Walton.

At night they went out and cruised around. Wheels were not a problem after Judi's three-year-older sister, Jill, took over the payments on their elder brother Jack's red-and-white '71 Olds Cutlass. They hit the Village Pizza Inn after the boys' games on Friday nights, and when there was no game they went downtown to the Lake Theatre to catch a movie.

The night the team went to see *Love Story*, there wasn't enough tissue for the whole squad. "Judi cried the whole time," says Cindy. "Everyone was snifflin' but Judi had to bite her thumb to keep from gettin' loud. We were all sentimental girls. By the end Judi had about bitten her thumbnail off. The girl dies. We ended up bawlin'. What else can you do?"

At school they were branded as "jocks." Girls snubbed them, and they felt the boys they knew best—mainly other athletes—were a little intimidated by their closeness to each other. They wore little makeup—maybe just a little blush, except for Margie Lozier, the manager, who was into mascara—and, as Cindy Ross put it, "It took at least a funeral to get us into a dress." They all had boyfriends off and on, but they weren't oriented toward dating, except around prom time. "I think right then we all got a little sweaty," remembers Cindy. "Everyone wanted to go to the prom."

"We weren't the ones the guys wanted to be with," Judi Warren recalls. "We weren't the cheerleaders and high-society girls all the other girls looked up to. It wasn't cool to date a jock. At times it was discouraging, but we weren't trying to impress anyone or stand out as a group. We just went out and had a good time.

"At that time, my teammates were closer to me than my own family. We knew each other very well. We understood each other. Our mental toughness kept us going. We became a unique group. We would do anything in the world for each other. We would do anything in the world to keep one of the others from going down."

Even though the girls had a team, basketball at Warsaw High meant boys' basketball. Warsaw High was a big county seat school with a winning tradition. The boys' basketball team filled the stands every home game and made enough money to pay for all the girls' programs and the rest of the boys' sports as well. As far as the athletic department was concerned, the girls should have been grateful they even *had* a team.

The girls saw it differently. Warsaw High was their school, too, and they didn't even have uniforms. They practiced in grade schools at inconvenient hours. And besides, going into their senior year they had lost only four games in three years. That was a lot better than the boys had done.

To the girls, the oppressor was Ike Tallman, the head boys' coach. Tall, broad and given to dark suits, he was an imposing figure. Having once won the state boys' tourney as a coach at Muncie Central High School only increased his stature and prominence. One evening after school Judi, Cindy and Lisa entered Warsaw's athletic office, their hearts hammering against their ribs. Lisa handed a list of demands to Tallman. They wanted uniforms and laundry service for them, buses for the games, cheerleaders and, above all, equal access to the Warsaw gym for practice.

Tallman studied the list for a while, then he looked up. Well, he said, to succeed you have to promote yourself. What you need is tickets. He told them that he'd have his secretary make up some orange tickets, the school's color, and the girls should see if they could sell enough of them to fill the gym. When they could fill the gym, like the boys did, why, then they could have it. Lisa, who had organized the event and written the list, grew livid. Cindy burst into tears.

When the secretary delivered the tickets, they didn't know what to do with them. They decided to try to sell them. Friends and relatives and people at church bought them faithfully, but few showed up at the games. This wasn't going to get them anywhere.

In their senior year the girls were granted permission to

Warsaw Tigers players lead their own cheers, 1976 championship game. *(Courtesy Indiana High School Athletic Association)*

The Tigers hold their championship trophy aloft—except for Judi Warren (center) who can barely reach it. Cindy Ross is at Judi's left. *(Courtesy Indiana High School Athletic Association)* (RIGHT)

Judi Warren magnified herself in concert, as all great performers do. At the end of the 1976 title game, she was at the line, swishing free throw after free throw.

(Courtesy Indiana High School Athletic Association)

Judi Warren drives against East Chicago Washington at Butler Field House. *(Warsaw* Times-Union)

practice in the gym after the boys were finished. It was a bittersweet victory. Judi lived too far away to go home for dinner and then return to the school for practice. Instead, she would stay in Warsaw, study for an hour or so at school and then stroll with Lisa to Burger's Dairy Store for a couple of jars of baby food. Somehow "Fruit Delight," a mixed fruit, had become the official training food of the Warsaw Tigers.

Then they'd walk back to watch the boys practice. Judi studied the drills carefully and tried them herself when the boys' practice was over. She found she could do anything they could except dribble between her legs on the run. At 5'1", her stride wasn't quite long enough for that.

It was usually 9:00 by the time practice was over. With luck, Jill would be waiting in the Cutlass. By the time she got home, Judi had just enough energy left to stumble into the shower and roll into bed.

"I can remember Judi coming home and telling me she had talked to the coach," says Janet Warren, "and I said, 'Judi, you shouldn't talk to your superiors like that.' Looking back, the girls knew what they were doing. I just wasn't in on it. What I knew was that she was never home because she was always at practice. That was kind of upsetting, because it's hard to work around a family when one member is gone so late. We are a family that likes to sit down and have our meals together. It was a sacrifice for everyone."

In 1975, the summer before the girls' senior year, the IHSAA took over the administration of the girls' basketball program and announced that the first girls' state tourney would be held that March. It would be just like the boys' tournament, with all teams in one tourney regardless of enrollment.

That same summer Cindy's dad, Bill Ross, died suddenly of a stroke. The girls were devastated. He had been a part of the team, a constant source of encouragement and cheer. Shattered, Cindy decided to quit the team. The others wouldn't hear of it. Cindy was the center, their rebounder, their enforcer, their intimidator.

But it was more than that: it was like losing a limb. "Judi and those guys said I couldn't quit because I was part of them. They said, 'We wouldn't know how to act without you.' We each knew what the others could do. They said, 'You gotta stay, for us.' So I decided to stay, and we started thinkin' that we could go to state and prove to people that we were legitimate athletes. We knew that having a dream wasn't good enough unless we worked and got it. My dream was to win the tourney to honor my father, because of the time he'd given me and what we'd done together." Together, they decided to win the first state championship for Bill Ross.

As the tourney approached, Cindy's life became even more complicated. She had fallen in love. Mike Knepper had asked her out that summer and they knew it was real almost from the start. But she had little time to see him and she wouldn't skip practice. It was a classic Hoosier conflict: love vs. training.

Faithful but lonesome, Mike would wander over to the Rosses' house and hang out with Cindy's mom and brothers until she came home from practice. Then they'd sink down onto the living room couch or go out for a quick drive. "This basketball is getting old, Cindy," Mike would say. "You never have time for us." And Cindy would throw an arm around him and soothe him with the words that Hoosier guys have used since 1911. "Mike," she would say, "the season won't last forever."

They were good, and Judi was the spark plug. She may have been only 5'1", but she was totally aggressive and jet-fast. She could pick your pocket and lay it in at the other end. The team's strategy was simply to outrun and wear down everyone else. They pressed from end to end and fast-broke at every occasion, with Judy penetrating and passing the ball off to Cindy, Lisa, Cathy Folk or a gifted sophomore athlete named Chanda Kline.

They entered the tournament undefeated, unknown and pitted against 350 other schools. Fifty or so relatives and close friends watched them win the sectional tournament. As the first sectional champs ever, they again demanded better uniforms and cheerleaders, just like the guys. The administration let the junior varsity cheerleaders go with them to the regional tournament.

When they won the regionals, the school began to take notice. Posters appeared in the halls. Kids began to stop at their lockers to wish them good luck. It felt weird but good. Judi was dating a guy already in college, and they all got a little misty when roses arrived after the regional title. "He was a jewel," recalls Judi's mom.

The fifty fans became 1,500 for the semistate. Hoosiers were Hoosiers, and this was one helluva basketball team, and it had been here right under their noses. Orange was the color, and the fans all wore orange T-shirts. The team blew through the semistate, too, and now there was real, high-voltage excitement. This was the first girls' tourna-

ment, after all, and the Bicentennial year. Warsaw's girls
could be pioneers.

One afternoon, in the week before the state finals, the
school held a pep rally for them. Lisa, Cindy, Judi, Chanda,
Cathy and the others sat in folding chairs in the middle of
the court, staring at this throng of their schoolmates who
a few weeks before wouldn't have passed up a dogfight to
see one of their games.

Toward the end, Ike Tallman rose to his feet and walked
slowly across the polished floor to the microphone. The
gym was silent. The girls had no idea what he was doing,
unless he was going to use *their* moment to remind everyone that the boys' tournament was starting soon.

For a moment he said nothing. Then, looking at Lisa,
he began, "Some of you have been after me to share this
gym and I said no, not until you can fill it. Well, I owe you
girls an apology." He paused and swept his hand in an arc
around the room. "Because now I see you *can* fill this gym."
Cindy Ross's voice breaks even today in telling that story.
"After that," she says, "we got a whole lot of respect for
him. It took a lot for the head coach of Warsaw to say he
was sorry to a bunch of girls."

Their first game in the state finals in Indianapolis was to
be against East Chicago Washington, all of whose players
except one was black. This was a totally new and forbidding
prospect for small-town girls who had encountered very
few black people.

The guys, now eager to help, reported that the typical
East Chicago crowd was a crazed mob given to tipping cars
over and setting them ablaze. Even more sobering were
accounts from the Rochester High girls who had lost to
them the week before. "Rochester told us that they would

205

probably draw knives on us," says Cindy. "We really believed it." But, said Rochester, they didn't just knife you
right away. They cussed you out first. Every dirty word in
the book.

Knives were one thing, but coach Janice Soyez was not
about to let her players become unnerved by dirty words,
not having gone this far. So they created a cussing drill in
practice, to simulate a game situation. Two girls, an offensive player and a defender, worked their way down and
back up the court. The defender had to cuss out the defensive player. "We didn't know what to say," recalls Cindy.
"We were all church-goin' girls. But we figured they'd call
us 'honky' all the time. So one would dribble and the other
would say, 'You bunch of damned honkies.' "

"Never having been around that many blacks, we didn't
know how to handle it," says Judi. "We had always looked
upon blacks as pretty rough people. We walked into the
game and we were thinkin', 'Oh, my God.' They were big
and they were black." They were also unarmed, business-
like and very good. East Chicago jumped off to a quick
eight-point lead, and Cindy committed three fouls in the
first two minutes. "I was astounded," Cindy says. "I thought,
'This has got to be wrong. This isn't how it was written.'
So we dug in deeper."

In the second quarter Judi got it going by stealing the
ball again and again, threading her way through defenses
and hooking passes over her head for easy baskets. Chanda
was hitting every shot she tried. Warsaw turned the game
around and opened up a big lead in the fourth quarter.

"They turned out to be good, aggressive players, nothing
short of that," recalls Cindy. "They really didn't talk to us
at all. . . . Color didn't make any difference at all." After
the game, Warsaw tried to walk over and shake hands, but

officials intercepted the girls from both teams and herded them downstairs and into their locker rooms.

Over 5,000 people had seen the game, nearly half of them from Warsaw. Just as important, hundreds of thousands of Hoosiers had flicked on the TV. Probably many of them had intended to watch for just a moment, to see what girls playing basketball looked like. Given the strong ratings that game drew, lots of them must have taken their hands off the dial and sat down to watch it. That little gal with the short hair could sure hustle. Kinda like Bill Keller or Billy Shepherd or Monte Towe. Hundreds decided to drive on out to Hinkle Field House for the championship game.

That night, when the team burst out of the dressing room and up the stairs, down through the hall behind the bleachers at Hinkle Field House where Oscar Robertson had run before taking the floor against Gary Roosevelt, where Bobby Plump had hit his shot, the tradition of it all, the cameras, the 3,000 orange-shirted fans who had caravaned from Warsaw to see them go for it, gave them gooseflesh. It hit them all. This was it. This was for the state championship.

That night there were more than 9,000 people in the stands and a huge prime-time TV audience. The game, against Bloomfield, was close until the final minute. But again Judi took over at the end, slashing again and again down the lane, scoring or passing to Chanda for assists, drawing fouls and shooting free throws.

Though Judi Warren was the smallest player by far, she somehow magnified herself in concert, as all great performers do. It was plain to see that here, too, was Hoosier Hysteria, packaged differently but radiant and authentic. At the end she was on the line, hitting free throws one after another, pulling her hair, jumping up and down clapping, embracing her teammates, thrusting her fists in the air, shimmering like a hummingbird. This wasn't palm slaps and whacks on the butt, this was something new. These girls were excited, and they showed it. They led their own cheers during time-outs. That night Hoosierland melted into a big warm puddle.

When it was over and they had won, and Judi had won the Mental Attitude Award, and the last strands of the net had been snipped and all the cameras packed away, they slipped on their coveralls, climbed into the Winnebago van and headed home for some sleep. They hoped someone would be there to meet them.

The van pulled into the school lot at 3:00 A.M. When they drew the curtain back, they were looking at a cop. When they opened the door, he said, "Better run, I don't think we can hold them back any longer." They were slapped on the back and borne into the gym, which people had again filled for them, but this time completely, the stands, the floor and the halls leading in. No one in Warsaw had gone to bed. When Judi and Cindy hoisted up the trophy, the cheer shook the rafters. "You know what I was thinkin'?" says Cindy. "I was thinkin' I wouldn't get to play ball with these guys next week."

The tournament had netted $20,000. Girls' basketball was on the map. Commissioner Patricia Roy had been vindicated and had even won a steak dinner from her boss, Commissioner Phil Eskew, who had wagered that no more than 2,000 would show. Judi was in "Faces in the Crowd" in *Sports Illustrated*. She received thousands of letters, including more than a few mash notes. Each night for a month or two she'd come home late from tennis practice, sink into the tub and dictate responses to Jill, whom they called her "agent." Boys were everywhere now; some wanted to date her, others to challenge her to a game.

And the Tigers had their own rubber chicken circuit. Coach Soyez made them a social calendar at the beginning of each month. Kiwanis. Lions. Rotary. Tri Kappa. Judi was the DePauw University Parade Marshal. Janet must have been proud to see her on "Homemaker's Time," a noontime TV talk show.

To their astonishment, and to their parents' great relief, they started getting letters from colleges. The obsession was actually going to pay off. One small college offered scholarships to the four seniors, but only if they would all attend. A small college in Alaska offered scholarships to Judi and Cindy, but would agree to fly them back to Warsaw only once a year.

It was amazing. The year before, Judi had received a tart reply to her polite letter of inquiry about basketball scholarships at Indiana State University. "Don't reply if you're under six feet," the coach had written. Well, Judi had thought, that pretty well let her out.

And the haircut. Remember the haircut? The stylist shaped it into a bowl, turned under and maintained easily with a curling iron. "It just looked so cute," recalls her mother. After the tournament, scores of Hoosier girls climbed into barber chairs, demanding "the Judi cut."

Today Cindy, the mother of three, runs a women's club. Her eldest daughter, Autumn, says she wants to be a cheerleader. April, 3, "wants to play ball like mom." Lisa's dream had been to be the first woman Supreme Court justice. They were sure she would make it and a little disappointed when Sandra Day O'Connor edged her out. Lisa had a start as a paralegal up in Chicago, but, according to Cindy, "She found out she could make more money waitressin' in a bar.

She runs in marathons, too." Cathy Folk is with an orthopedics company down south and Chanda Kline is finishing up her master's in business administration: "You know how if you're tryin' to decide whether to put another McDonald's in Warsaw?" asks Cindy. "Well, Chanda does all the stat work."

Judi Warren is the coach of a girls' high school basketball team and the mother of a 4-year-old son. He can already dribble with both hands and heave a small ball through a hoop ten feet off the ground. "I get really excited about him," she says. "I hope someday he wants to play. I tell myself I'm not going to push him, but I'm going to make every opportunity available to him."

In her cinder-block office, Judi is reflective. A bell rings and kids thunder by. Locker doors clang shut. Another bell rings, and then the silence is total. "Without basketball," she says, "I don't know what I'd be doing . . . I'd probably be Holly Homemaker with about twenty kids running around." She laughs. "It would be totally different. I can't imagine it.

"When I was really young, when I was the only girl playin' with all the boys, Mom kept trying to tell me I was too much of a tomboy and I should try to change. She said that until there just wasn't anything she could do about it and she gave in. Then she said she was kind of a tomboy, too, maybe not as much as me. She said she always used to tease the boys. But I wasn't doin' it to tease them, and I didn't do it to impress anybody. I never tried to be anyone else . . . I did it because I loved the game."

LARRY BIRD:

Peace

in

the Valley

Larry Bird shuffles into the lobby of the Grand Hyatt, all glass and mirrors on 42nd Street and Lexington Avenue in midtown Manhattan, head down, wearing an enormous kelly green baseball jacket, nondesigner jeans and pointy western boots. He is in New York to do a Converse commercial, the one where Magic materializes from behind him and Dr. J.

Bird is traveling with First Sergeant T. A. Hill of the Indiana State Police and two admen, a redhead who is clearly in charge and his sandy-haired attaché. The admen have only one assignment—to deliver Bird, Magic and Dr. J. to the film crew at eight the next morning. Magic is already safely in his room and this Dr. J.—a responsible-seeming type—is driving in from Philly in the morning. So they stick with Bird, who is said to be somewhat independent.

Bird and Hill throw their bags in their room and head down to the Trumpet Room for a bite. The admen are waiting at the table. Bird and Hill are greeted by the headwaiter, a correct man of perhaps half Bird's mass, who informs them that a jacket is required in the Trumpet Room. Words are exchanged, some of them not commonly heard there. "Let's get the hell out of here," says Bird to Hill, and they turn and vanish into the night. It is 10:00 P.M.

The fullness of what has just happened seems to hit Red in phases. The thoughts come something like this:

1. The man more men would like to buy a beer than anyone is loose in midtown Manhattan, unmistakable at 6'9".
2. He is out there with an Indiana state trooper; God knows if the guy is armed or how short his fuse might be.
3. This is a $275,000 account.
4. To summarize, he has probably blown a relatively simple and very big assignment.

When this circuitry is complete, Red leaps to his feet and charges the headwaiter, confronting him chest to chest. Does he realize who that was? No. Does he *know* how much Converse spends in Hyatt hotels? Doesn't seem to.

Finally, the waiter seems to realize that he has made some kind of massive mistake and asks what he can do to atone. The question catches Red cold. Other diners are craning. The scene is deteriorating. Bird and Hill are melting deeper into the naked city by the moment. Backing out of the room, Red levels the little guy with a hard stare and a pointed finger, and gives him the only order he can think of: You'd *better* have a bottle of your best champagne in the room of one Magic Johnson by the time I get back.

Larry Bird dresses like a truck driver, talks like a frontiersman and draws back a huge fist when you push him too far. His humor has a hard edge. He has old ways: He plays hurt and doesn't whine about it. He hunts and fishes and drinks beer and probably smells like a man after a workout. It wouldn't surprise anyone to see a thermos and pail in his locker.

He is a Hoosier and proud of it, the kind of man that modern Indianapolis seems to be trying to forget, the woodsman-cum-farmer-cum-time-card-puncher. He is an image from Indiana's past, back when language and movement and speech were direct, when basketball was all there was in the winter and when it was played best by white guys from Hoosier towns, guys who spent more time on the floor than in the air.

"I really don't need anyone to boost my ego," Larry Bird has said. "I've already proven that a white boy who can't run and jump can play this game." Of course that had always been assumed in Indiana, at least until the '50s, when black players began to fly away with the game. After a long period of adjustment, Hoosier coaches learned to neutralize speed and leaping ability by slowing the game down. Today, Hoosiers have once again become used to championship high school teams with few black players. Still, nobody ever expected the best player in the world to look like Larry Bird again.

There are already streets in French Lick and Terre Haute that bear his name. After he held up the NBA championship trophy on national TV and said, "This is for Terre Haute," they tried to wipe the donor's name right off the Indiana State University Field House and put his up there instead. He stopped it with a letter to the local newspaper.

Still, as they pour out their hearts in thanksgiving, Hoosiers ask: Who *is* this guy? He may be the best player in the world, but his team never even got out of the Bedford regional. He was invisible on the all-star team, they say.

And what makes him so good? He certainly is a weird kind of superstar. They say he wins with his head, but he sure doesn't talk like a genius. Can you teach this "floor presence" and "court awareness" everybody talks about?

How do you teach your kid to think two steps faster than everyone else? The gyroscope he has in his head, the thing that lets him calculate relative velocities and distances like a falcon tracking down a dove, where do you get one of those? More to the point: How did Larry Bird get that way?

French Lick and West Baden, Indiana, are two sides of the same road sign, along Highway 56, in a valley to which Indians and white settlers alike were drawn by three springs of rank-tasting, foul-smelling waters that their animals seemed to love. This is the hill country of southern Indiana, springs and limestone quarries and fossil beds, the part that was piled up by the last glacier to come through.

In 1904 Thomas Taggart, mayor of Indianapolis, a genial Irishman who was doubtless cheered by the few cents he and his cronies made on every barrel of beer sold in Indiana, built a 600-room resort hotel and mineral spa in the valley and named it the French Lick Springs Hotel. Located at the junction of the Southern and Monon railroads, it became one of America's preeminent resorts.

Twenty-one trains a day carried socialites and industrialists, politicians and entertainers, prizefighters and gamblers and gangsters through southern Indiana and right up to the portico. There they were met by some of the more than one hundred black porters and busmen, who wheeled their trunks over the sawdust walking paths, past the Japanese gardens and into the great hotel itself.

They checked in, found their rooms and went down to the baths, Turkish baths, Russian baths, electric baths, mud baths, expensive baths full of the same stuff the Indians' horses had lapped up. Taggart called it "Pluto" water, after the king of the underworld.

Taggart built a bottling plant across the street and soon was selling Pluto water hand over fist. Pluto's twenty-two minerals were said to soften skin, cure rheumatism and arthritis and clean the pores. And, especially after even more salts were added, it won rightful acclaim as a laxative. Guests found a jar of Pluto outside their doors each morning. "If nature won't, Pluto will," said the label.

Leaders from all professions gathered there. Al Capone, the Pluto of his day, was a regular guest; he was perhaps the only one who relaxed with five bodyguards. It is a Bird family story that Big Al once tipped Larry Bird's grandfather a hundred dollars. The hotel was a popular site for political conventions. In 1904, Democratic National Chairman Tom Taggart ran Judge Alton B. Parker's faltering campaign against Teddy Roosevelt from the hotel lobby. In the same grand setting, the nation's governors squeezed Al Smith out in 1931 and brought in FDR as the party's new standard-bearer.

Tom Taggart took womb-to-tomb care of valley residents. Almost everyone who lived in the valley worked either at the hotels—a rival sprang up in West Baden—or at the Pluto plant. Taggart built separate housing for the black workers who came up from Evansville and Louisville. They had their own church and school, their own restaurant and bar in the "Brown building." Even Joe Louis, who trained for several of his fights at the West Baden Hotel, was not allowed to stay in the rooms, although he alone among blacks was allowed to play on the French Lick Springs golf course.

Whites ran the grounds, the kitchen, the golf course and the casinos. They worked year-round, nine hours a day. In the winter, they stayed outdoors, clearing ice off the trees. During the summer, the women who did not work in the dining halls got ready for winter, freezing meats, canning, getting the apples in. Three generations of people in the valley slipped out of their beds and into uniforms each morning and made ready to coddle the richest people on earth. It is small wonder that Larry Bird, the grandson of Tom Taggart's people, feels no particular qualms about striding through the world's finest hotels in jeans.

The winter rivalry between the West Baden Sprudels and the French Lick Red Devils was red-hot even by Hoosier standards. Both towns were poor and small, and there was no breathing space between them. "They just despised each other," says Jack Carnes, 52, a lifelong valley resident who today heads the kitchen of the French Lick Springs Hotel. "You were just liable to get beat up if you went to West Baden or a West Baden kid went to French Lick. They fought over that basketball *all* the time.

"When I was a kid growin' up, there probably wasn't a ball game when there wasn't a fight afterwards. Our teams weren't that good, but whether you won or lost, you *had* to agitate the other team. The old West Baden gym had a balcony with four or five rows of seats, and I've seen people jump off of that balcony and onto a player. It was just *violent*."

In the mid-'50s the two towns began to face pressure from the State Board of Education to consolidate their schools. West Badenites could see the writing on the wall from the start, for theirs was the smaller school.

In a series of rancorous public hearings, they first resisted the whole idea, then fought for a new building which would straddle the town line. But French Lick had almost 80 percent of the valley's people and almost all the power.

Well, they said, one thing was sure. They were damned if their kids were going to play for, root for or date French Lick Red Devils. So it was that in the fall of 1957, when the West Baden kids crossed the line into French Lick, they went not as Red Devils, but as Springs Valley High Black Hawks.

The first Springs Valley basketball team must have been sent from heaven. Even today, valley residents invoke the boys of '58 as the Irish recall cherished rebellions. They won twenty-five games in a row. In the tourney, they massacred three teams from big schools, teams ranked among the top ten in Indiana. It actually looked like they might go all the way, until they were martyred in the state finals by Fort Wayne South, who had a 7'-tall center.

Residents make it clear that it was the *team*, not the board of education, that consolidated the schools. They buried the hatchet in the skulls of common foes. Some of the players were from French Lick and some from West Baden, but when sharpshooters like Bob McCracken and Marvin Pruett started lobbin' mortar from the corners and the fast break was on, there were no Sprudels or Red Devils, only Black Hawks and enemies. Such was the heat that coach Rex Wells, who had come from West Baden, spent much of his time calming his players. At halftime, he would sit the boys down, pass out oranges and read them poetry.

Tickets became harder to come by as the undefeated string grew longer. The shortage became a drought, a matter that naturally engaged civic leaders like Shorty Rennert, who owned the poolroom downtown. "We was all in there one night, gripin' about how we couldn't get into the Shawswick game," recalls Jack Carnes. "Next night Shorty had tickets for everyone, good seats, too. He said, 'Only thing is, be there when the doors open.' We thought it was funny that he didn't wanna go.

"Well, we got in first thing and before long some people came in wantin' our seats. We got in a big fuss, the police friskin' everybody, and finally they set up new seats for us on the floor. When we got back we told him all about it and Shorty said, 'I knew I didn't get the color quite right.' "

Today a great banner celebrating the Team of '58, one of the best teams ever seen in southern Indiana, hangs from the rafters of the Springs Valley gym. "If we'd had a losing season that year," says Jack Carnes, "we'd probably still be fightin' today."

The Birds, Kerns and Nobles settled into the valley mainly from Ireland and Wales. Joe and Georgia Bird, married when Joe came back from Korea, produced six children, five boys and a girl.

Larry, born in 1956, was the third of five boys. Like lots of younger brothers, Larry grew up fast, tagging along, younger and smaller, burning to play too. "When me and Mike were 8 and 9, Larry was 4 or 5," says Larry's brother Mark. "Every time we went someplace, we had to take him along. We used to beat him up every day. He was a little smart butt. We used to send him home cryin' and then Dad'd come down there and beat me 'n' Mike up for beatin' up his baby. He'd come down with a switch or somethin', and me and Mike'd get it. Even if we just told him he couldn't play, he'd go home and tell Dad we hit him, and it'd be all over for us."

"Those brothers were so competitive, and they just pounded on the kid," says Jim Jones, the Springs Valley coach when Larry was growing up. "Boy, he'd fight them tooth and nail, and he'd stay around and play after they'd leave. His will to win was the biggest thing. I remember in Little League, when he'd get beat he'd cry. They were just great, competitive kids."

Larry started his career on a basketball team in fourth grade. He is remembered locally as a skinny kid with a good eye and a quick temper. Once in junior high he was sent home from practice for fighting.

The family had a hard time making ends meet. They moved around a lot, sometimes living with relatives in the country. When he started playing for the school teams, Larry moved in with his grandmother, as Mike and Mark had done when they played. She lived only a block from the school, and, better still, she let the boys stay out as late as they wanted. Larry would play in the gym at night until they locked the doors and then play outdoors. "I used to drive by the park, and he'd be out there with a couple of friends until one or two in the morning," says Gary Holland, then Jones's assistant coach. Even after the others went home, Larry would stay out, whipping the ball against a concrete wall.

Larry made the Springs Valley team as a sophomore, wearing Mark's old number, 33. A guard, he stood 6'1" and weighed but 135 pounds. Jones had long been aware of Larry's special intuition for the game. "Even in junior high," says Jones, "he would let his man go and steal the ball from someone else. He could just anticipate what someone else was going to do. He just picked it up so much faster than anyone else."

In the season's second game, Larry broke his ankle in a battle for a rebound. He practiced shooting with the team until his cast came off and begged Jones for a chance to play again. "We told him if he could play up to a certain level, we'd take him to the state tournament," says Jones. "I didn't tell him we'd already decided to take him. He practiced very hard, dragged his leg around. He'd have to run the suicide drill every day within a certain time, and he couldn't do it and get frustrated and almost cry." He went to the tournament, got himself in at the end of a close game and won it with two free throws.

He had a fine junior year as a 6'3" guard, averaging about sixteen points, ten rebounds and six assists a game and helping a senior named Steve Land break the school scoring record. Many around town were beginning to think he might have a future as a small college guard.

No one was prepared for what happened. Over the summer, Larry shot up to 6'7" and increased his strength by working out each day on the football team's new Universal weight machine. Somehow he lost none of his exceptional coordination; instead, overnight, he became a guard in a center's body.

"I had been away at college, and I hadn't seen him play," recalls Mark Bird. "Once between his junior and senior years I was workin' with our uncle up in Gary and Larry and a friend came up to see us. Suddenly he was 6'6" and he'd put on some weight. I couldn't believe it."

Basketball had become his life. There is no reference to Larry Bird in his senior yearbook that does not relate to basketball, no clubs or prom pictures or senior trips, not even other sports. "Larry never paid much attention to girls growing up," says John ("Beeser") Carnes, Larry's high school teammate and constant companion. "He was basketball-minded."

Beeser describes a typical Saturday during basketball season: "I'd probably stay all night with Larry. We'd sleep in till about noon and Larry'd like to talk about who we were gonna play that night. You couldn't keep him from talking about basketball. Then his granny—he has the most wonderful granny—would fix lunch and we'd go out and ride around." They didn't smoke or drink, says Beeser, and those with drugs "knew not to come around us." At night, they hit the drive-in or hung around the Shell station or shot pool at Shorty's. As Beeser puts it, "We were just typical kids."

Larry Bird's senior year at Springs Valley had to be as good a year as any Indiana player has ever had, but, because Larry played in a remote part of southern Indiana, he received little statewide attention. Bird averaged about thirty-one points, twenty-one rebounds and five assists per game and led the team in every other statistical category but free-throw percentage. He twice scored over fifty points and once pulled down thirty-eight rebounds in a thirty-two-minute game.

That year, Jim Jones quit coaching to become the Springs Valley athletic director—"one of the many, many mistakes I've made in coaching," he says—and Gary Holland took over. Holland had grown up in Paoli, ten miles away, where he had been a basketball star. "My father still owns a store in Paoli," Holland says. "That first year, they shot his windows through with buckshot. I got calls in the night all winter long, people from Paoli saying 'Traitor' and hanging up."

Holland inherited from Jones a team of fast, good athletes, and he simply turned them loose. "It was probably the most fun year I've had," says Holland. "I figured, 'If it's gonna be like this, coaching's gonna be great.'"

Eddie Bird, the youngest of the five Bird brothers, at the free-throw line for the Springs Valley Black Hawks.

(Tom Roach)

French Lick Springs Hotel waiters, 1930s. *(Courtesy French Lick Springs Hotel)*

Make my day: the Springs Valley Black Hawks of 1974.
Larry Bird holds the ball. Beeser Carnes is number 35
(seated). *(Randy Dieter,* Sunday Courier and Press)

The former Monon Avenue, downtown French Lick. *(Tom Roach)*

Indiana high school all-star Larry Bird dunks against a Kentucky counterpart. Note the placement of Bird's left foot. Who needs to jump if you can think that fast? *(Courtesy Indianapolis Star)* (**LEFT**)

Larry's passing ability could be dangerous. "We used to tell them, 'Better have your head up, lookin' toward Larry,'" says Holland. "Even in high school, he made an average player great." "The man could do everything," says Beeser Carnes, who, having played on teams with Larry since fourth grade, has probably caught more of Larry's passes than anyone else. "He was the most unselfish man I ever played with. He could've scored any time he wanted to."

Asked if there was a single play that foreshadowed the Larry Bird of today, Holland, Mark Bird and Beeser Carnes all mention the same pass. Against Corydon High, on a night when he scored fifty-four points, Bird was in the left lane on a fast break. He was racing toward the corner when a teammate lofted a pass to him from the opposite side of the court. It came down a little behind him. Instead of slowing down to catch the ball, Bird reached back and batted the ball behind his back with his left hand, sending it on one bounce to Doug ("Turkey") Conrad, who was streaking down the middle and who laid it in without breaking stride. The next morning, Holland, Beeser, Larry and several others ran the film clip over and over. "We just sat there laughing," says Holland. "Even Larry had to laugh."

Larry's self-confidence increased by the game. "Frankly," says Beeser, "I always figured Gary wanted me to be the leader, but after the second or third game it was clear who our leader was. Larry liked to joke around, but it was always *after* practice. He'd get his work done first. He could come down on you out there, too. I might be standin' around and Larry'd come over and say, 'You tired? Then why aren't you workin' helpin' us win?'"

On the days when the team had a 6:30 A.M. free-throw practice, Jones would swing by Larry's grandmother's house and try to wake Larry and Beeser up. "Larry probably didn't look too favorably on it, but he'd roll out and put his pants on and we were off." Beeser, on the other hand, often rolled back over.

It came back to haunt him. In their senior tourney after Springs Valley had won the sectional, Beeser found himself on the line for four last-minute free throws against Bedford with the regional championship at stake. He missed them all, and Springs Valley lost by three points. "After the game," Beeser says, "we went back to Shorty's, and Larry just laid it out to me. He said, 'Beeser, you should have got up and shot them free throws in the mornings.' "

It didn't take long for Gary Holland to realize that there couldn't be many better players in Indiana, if any, and he owed it to Larry to spread the word. In Indiana, the greatest honor a boy can get is to be named "Mr. Basketball," and, after that, to make the twelve-player all-star team that has played a group of all-stars from Kentucky each summer since 1939. The selections are made by the Indianapolis *Star*, particularly by a promotions man named Don Bates. "When you die," explains Bates, "that's in your obit, that you were an Indiana All-Star. And it's usually in the lead paragraph. It's like your pedigree."

Bates and his advisory committee have a tough job. Half the coaches in Indiana are out to convince him they have an all-star. The lobbying is year-round and intense, with letter-writing campaigns and violent fan reactions when their boys don't make it. Always, fans from both northern and southern Indiana have believed the *Star* has slighted— maybe persecuted—them.

With Larry, Holland knew he had an uphill fight. "Mr. Basketball" was out of the question—no one would believe he was that good. Larry had been a guard the year before, the number-two scorer on a team that hadn't even won its sectional. Now he was a 160-pound center on a small, rural team, light-years from Indianapolis.

Holland called Jerry Birge, a respected sportswriter from nearby Jasper, who had seen Larry enough to know. Birge responded by printing hundreds of fliers and glossy action photos. He sent them to every newspaper and radio station in Indiana and hounded Don Bates and his colleagues at the *Star*. Birge had the feeling he was getting nowhere.

But early in the season Indiana University coach Bobby Knight began to show up at Larry's games. He'd slip in quietly, after the game had started, sit up there eating popcorn for a while and slip out again. He rarely spoke to Holland, or to Bird, but after the tourney, when he made his pitch, Larry signed. "We were all IU fans," says Mark Bird. "My dad was probably the biggest IU fan ever. He'd say to Larry, 'Boy, I seen this red jacket the other day, and I sure would like to buy it and wear it to one of your ball games.' "

"When he signed with IU, it really caught my attention," says Don Bates. "I thought, I'd better drive down and take a look at this kid. They were playing at Mitchell. I got there and they were warming up. Right away you could tell which one Bird was, shooting layups and jump shots. He had great hands, big hands. He scored about thirty-five points and had about twenty rebounds that night."

Larry made the all-star team, but, even after spectacular practices, he played less than half the time. When his coach summoned him for action at the end of the second game, he refused to play, stating that he wasn't a mop-up player. Deeply proud and certain of his abilities, he was burned by the insult, and the memories still linger.

Asked by writer Ray Didinger in 1985 to explain "What do you think it is that drives you?" Bird replied, "I'm sure it dates back to Indiana . . . I didn't even make all-state my senior year [he didn't make the wire service teams] . . . I heard what they said about me. Too slow, can't jump. Country kid, never had the big-city competition. I went to the state all-star game my senior year, and I got in the first five minutes. I wondered if I was really that bad.

"I look back and I realize I was the best player in the state. No one gave me credit for it. But maybe it worked out for the best. It kept me practicing four or five hours a day in the summer, and now it's a habit."

Today Springs Valley High School is located at 101 Larry Bird Boulevard, a thoroughfare whose origin is marked by a fifteen-foot-tall orange basketball-shaped sign with Larry's name on it. Entering the gym by the front door, on the night of a game between Springs Valley High and the Washington Hatchets, you walk past a trophy case containing Larry's Indiana All-Star jersey and down into the Black Hawks' nest.

The gym seats 2,800—except when they wedged in 4,000 for Larry's last home game. The room can hold the combined population of French Lick and West Baden and is quite adequate for Springs Valley 296 students. This gym, which has no other purpose but basketball, would be the biggest high school gym in more than a few states, but there are at least 150 others in Indiana that seat even more.

The walls bear framed photos of the great teams, the Team of '58, the regional champs of '64 and the five sectional champs. Staring down on the whole room from over the main entrance, as his little brother Eddie warms up, is the enlarged image of Larry Bird.

An impressive number of students are involved in this midweek game. Springs Valley's cheering block is large and there is a thunderous band with a formidable tuba section. Most of the students are dressed in cotton shirts, jeans and sneakers. Some girls are busy tucking strands of angora yarn into the gap between their left-hand third finger and their boyfriends' oversized class rings. "I always go for younger guys," says Tammi Rausch, a senior, fingering the ring of Roger Allen, a junior, who plays on the reserve team but dresses varsity. "Most girls around here date college guys. Around here, girls are more mature."

Larry has been good to the school. He makes sure that fifty balls and fifty pairs of new shoes arrive at the gym each year. "You can't believe how helpful that is," says Gary Holland. "Besides the money we save, every time a kid here picks up a new ball, he thinks, 'Larry Bird.' That means hard work and dedication." In Larry's honor, the number 33—which no Black Hawk will ever wear again— is stitched to each reserve team warmup jacket.

This year's squad is like a younger generation of Larry's team. "It's amazing," says Gary Holland. "I have a Bird, a Carnes, a Land and a Rominger." Eddie Bird, the last of the six Bird children and a senior at Springs Valley High, plays the wing on the Black Hawks' 2–3 zone and center on offense. He does not have the recognition problem Larry had. He averaged about twenty points per game as a junior and has made most of the preseason all-state teams. Magazine articles point out that Eddie has a chance—if he averages about twenty-three points—to break Larry's school scoring record. Eddie has already received recruiting letters from forty or so colleges, some of them for baseball.

Eddie has the ball a lot of the time. He clearly is a good athlete, a good ball handler, with a fine, arching jump shot and nice moves to get free. He has soft, curly brown hair and a faint moustache. Like Larry, Eddie spends a good bit of time at rest rubbing the bottoms of his tennis shoes. Mark does this, too, while he is coaching the seventh-grade team, as do his young players. So do all the members of the Black Hawk varsity. It has become the community nervous tic.

At least in this game, Eddie Bird does not seem to be a man of the trenches. At times he plays a beat behind, a little distracted, it seems, content to leave the boards to teammate Mike Land, who lunges for nearly every rebound available. At the end of the third quarter, as Springs Valley overtakes the Hatchets and begins to pull away, the game degenerates. Eddie hangs back for breakaway passes, misses one dunk and then slams another home.

Mark Bird, standing near the door, arms folded across a powder-blue sweater, is not impressed. Mark's team photo is up on that wall too, from when he was a high-scoring guard for a sectional champion. He was a better free-throw shooter than Larry; in fact, Mark never missed a free-throw in a tourney game.

"He's not hungry," Mark says, eyes straight ahead. "Gary ought to bench him, that'd set him straight." Eddie again breaks toward his offensive basket as a teammate swipes for the ball. "He's cherry pickin'," says Mark, disgusted. "He wants to dunk. He should have played more this summer 'stead of settin' around." Mark, whom Gary Holland describes as the most competitive of the Bird brothers, is not willing to concede Eddie second place in the family hierarchy, at least not if the kid doesn't want it. "I sure wish I'd had his height when I was a senior," Mark says.

Things are different in the valley now. Pluto water stopped selling in the mid-'30s, a decade before the state police came in and boarded up the casinos. Shortly before he was murdered by a Capone mob member in Arkansas, the owner of the West Baden Springs Hotel donated it to a Catholic order.

But the French Lick Sheraton, as it is now called, is back on the upswing after decades of musty decline. Each day in the Pluto Room, Richard, an Indiana University student recently from Great Britain, gives a mean thirty-minute Pluto massage, kneading the twenty-two minerals through all seven layers of skin for only $7.50.

Politicians still come: Nixon and Agnew, Ronald Reagan when he was governor of California. One morning in the late '60s Jack Carnes's pot washer walked out of the freight elevator, a vessel apparently overlooked by the Secret Service, and was startled to find Hubert Humphrey alone, writing, in the hotel kitchen.

When the Taggarts sold out, the towns had to grow up quickly. The Pluto plant, where Mark Bird now works, today turns out bottles of Blue Lustre Carpet Cleaner. The Kimball Organ Company has developed a scholarship program to try to keep kids in the valley. Still, many of those who leave for college settle in Terre Haute, Bloomington, Louisville or Indianapolis.

The sports rivalries remain hotter in the valley than in most parts of Indiana. Like New England, where you go to school means a lot in Orange County. This year the Black

Hawks finally felt things had simmered down enough to resume their rivalry with Dubois High, two towns over, after a quarter-century's athletic estrangement.

Larry Bird's success means a great deal to the morale and pride of the valley. His Celtic games are carried locally by satellite, and the Springs Valley *Herald* carries a "Bird-watch" column to chronicle his NBA feats. Everyone hopes he will come home to live after his career is over, but no one is sure, now that he's seen the world.

He returns each summer, staying in the splendid house he had built for his mother. Set in a huge front lawn is what basketball courts must look like in heaven, a patch of asphalt shimmering against the hills, with glass backboards, flood-lights and a gravel apron around the court. Sometimes in the summer he brings other Celtics for scrimmages with Eddie and the Black Hawks by day and high-stakes bass fishing tournaments when it cools down. "He even competes when you fish," observes Gary Holland.

At the Jubil Bar in West Baden, or at the Legion Hall, two of Larry's favorite spots when he comes home, the stories are thick, stories about the guy who hasn't changed, who picked up his first MVP trophy in jeans and left it on his mom's refrigerator, about the man who told the execs from the "American Sportsman" to call him back when they decided to fish the farm ponds of southern Indiana.

The people who know—or knew—Larry Bird best struggle like everyone else to explain the origin and nature of his genius. Nobody claims to have predicted Larry's success; even in a valley full of good storytellers, what happened is just too far-fetched. "We just didn't know what we had here," says Gary Holland. "He took all our drills and mastered them," says Jim Jones, "but he could utilize them on a much higher plane than anyone else. He'd make passes that you didn't even see were possible. You wondered, how'd *he* see them?"

Mark Bird holds to at least a partial genetic theory. "We were all good shooters," he says, "everyone in our family. They say that grandad Bird was just a tremendous baseball player. Dad quit school early to join the Navy, but Shorty Rennert knew our dad real well, and he'd say, 'You kids *ought to* be good, as good as your dad was.'"

After the standard observations about competitiveness and good vision and superior work habits, Gary Holland says something quite different, something that speaks to Larry's success in the NBA. "Larry just seemed like he could adjust to the character of other people," he says. "Really, the game of basketball is getting along with other players. After he got out of high school here he signed at IU, and then he dropped out and enrolled in Northwood Institute up here for a while. We never had any blacks in school for him to play with, but at Northwood there were a few, some good players. I was amazed how he could adjust to their style of play. It was rough play. He fit in real good. They really respected him."

Jack Carnes thinks it over for a while in the hotel kitchen. "Aw, it's just a miracle, really," he says.

"I don't think French Lick'll ever change," says Mark Bird, "but Larry's changed a little bit. I would say Larry's gotten a lot smarter since he left college as far as some of the other aspects of life. Now it seems like he's got so much on his mind, he's always late for somethin'. He just can't do much anymore. He used to be so outgoing, especially when he was in college. We'll all want him to go to St.

Louis for a baseball game and he won't want to fight the crowd and hassle. Now he'll go out to eat sometimes and people'll just hound him. That's out of French Lick. Here, nobody'll even bother him."

"I only got to see Larry once last summer," says Beeser Carnes, who today works as a pipefitter. "He just called me up and said, 'Let's go.' I don't always go, but that night I went. We just went out and drove around till four in the morning. I had to get up at five the next morning and I wanted to get one hour's sleep, anyway. He tried to talk me into cuttin' work the next day, but I have a mortgage on a new house I'm tryin' to pay off and I really couldn't cut . . . I told him, 'If you'll pay for the day,' and he just laughed."

Asked what Larry Bird is like, Beeser takes a long time to answer. "Larry's just Larry," Beeser says finally. "I can't describe him. I'll say I don't get to see enough of him. I'd just say it's a privilege to know him."

10

HOOSIER COACHES:

From
Bobby Knight
to
the Lady Lions

"What does every boy in this town want to be? He wants to be the basketball coach. It's the dream of the U.S.A.; the prairie wagon and the plains; the unconquerable frontier. That's why you stick with it; that's why coaches stay with the game."
—FROM JOHN R. TUNIS'S 1944 NOVEL
Yea! Wildcats,
ABOUT LIFE IN KOKOMO, INDIANA

Mark Simmerman was ecstatic. His young Greenfield Central team had won the first game of its sectional. It looked like they might even win the whole thing for the first time in over thirty years.

Privately, he hoped the victory had saved his job, too. But given the nature of his one-year coaching contract, it wasn't crystal-clear: "They [the principal and athletic director] gave me a list with about fourteen or fifteen items that I needed to meet," says Simmerman. "One of them was that I had to win ten games." He had finished the regular season 9–11. This tournament victory was the tenth.

All season long Simmerman had tried to keep his situation from his players, but you don't keep secrets like that in a small town. Even the kids in the cheer block knew, for Simmerman's wife, Teri, also a teacher at the school, had been their faculty sponsor. "The whole cheer block was crying," says Teri Simmerman. "Our minister was there, and the next day he preached about it. The team captain came up to me afterward and said, 'Do I get a hug?' because he thought Mark's job had been saved."

Greenfield Central went on to win the sectional that evening, and it looked even better. But shortly after Greenfield lost the first game of the regional by three points to a New Castle team that went to the state finals, the principal and athletic director asked Mark Simmerman to resign. Ten wins was ten wins, and Simmerman had won nine. He refused to quit.

When the students heard, ninety-two of them walked out of school, chanting Simmerman's name. They marched to the local newspaper and asked for an investigation. Anguished, Simmerman tried to figure out what to do. Mostly, he thought about his coaching future. "In Indiana," he says, "some people think if you get fired there is something the matter, that there is something to it." Finally he scribbled "I quit" on a scrap of paper and handed it to the athletic director. Shortly after, local sportswriters named him County Coach of the Year.

At least the ordeal was over. "On nights when he would lose a game," says Teri Simmerman, "we'd be up till three or four in the morning because we knew what it meant. You see, I wasn't married to him when I first saw him coach. I didn't know what a coach went through. He was only 27 years old and he had higher blood pressure than my mother, who's on medicine."

"What it boiled down to," says Simmerman, "I'd made

two or three bigwigs upset. I'd made enough enemies because one kid didn't make the ball club or didn't play enough, and his dad would go and complain to the administration and they would listen to these people. The simplest thing [for them] was to make a change." He echoes a very familiar theme. "If they would just leave it up to the kids, there wouldn't be any problem. When the parents step in, there are problems."

The average high school basketball coach in Indiana lasts less than three years with a team. Two Indiana high schools began this season with their seventh head coach in the last eleven years.

Some Indiana school boards have the power to hire and fire only two individuals, the principal and the head basketball coach. It is common for Hoosiers to run for the school board for no other reason than to fire the coach.

"Corydon was the damnedest town I ever saw for hiring and firing coaches," says former IHSAA Commissioner Phil Eskew. "I remember talking to the superintendent down there, who said, 'I think we got it all fixed up now. We're going to rehire both the football and basketball coach. I think I'll get that done tonight.' I had breakfast with him the next morning. He said, 'Damnedest thing happened last night. I went into that meeting and someone made a motion: 'I move we fire the basketball coach.' It was carried. Then someone else said, 'Well, I move we fire the *football* coach,' and he was gone. That was the school board."

The tenure is shaky, the pressures volcanic, the pay minimal and the hours eternal. And yet, each vacancy is eagerly sought in Indiana. Why would anyone want to coach? Same reason someone would want to be a rabbi in Williamsburg, a cowboy in Wyoming, a guide in the Adirondacks, a county agent in Iowa, a conductor in Vienna or a claims adjustor in Hartford. Coaching is the operative profession in the community, the way to participate most directly in the experience of Indiana.

A good basketball coach is a conspicuous, respected, consulted and admired community leader, a source of power. The rewards are visibility, respect and a chance to shape the most vital aspects of a community. For some, it's a chance to stay young, to stay with a game you love and played and don't want to leave.

"If you're good, a coach is just another minister," says Howard Sharpe, who has coached Indiana high school teams for forty-seven years. "The coach is the most crucified man in the community. You got to win. People don't know that every time there's a game there's a loser. The wife can't even go to the store if you don't win."

Indeed, a coach's wife has a lot in common with a preacher's wife. Mary Jo McCracken, wife of the late Indiana University coach Branch McCracken, recalled her awakening to writer Ray Marquette. "When Mac and I were first engaged, my father called me into his office one day and asked me point-blank what qualifications I had to be a good coach's wife. He told me that the university had a fine young basketball coach and he didn't want his career to be impaired. So we sat there for four hours and discussed how I could help Mac in his profession. I honestly believe that my father was more interested in Mac's future than he was in his daughter's ability to be a wife."

Coaches dread the day the son of the principal or superintendent tries out for the team, but even more harrowing can be the debut of the coaches' own progeny. "They booed our son one year," says Susan Held, wife of Anderson

High coach Norm Held. "I'll never forget that, although my son says he never heard it. I couldn't believe people would do such a thing. The year before, he had made the winning basket in the regional. It really bothered me."

A good coach can mean a great deal to a teenager. Coaches get a chance to make difficult things fun, to dramatize the value of cooperation, to attack self-doubt. The mere act of unlocking the gym early in the morning or late at night or in the summer can mean worlds, especially to poor kids. "I've fed my players, bought them clothes, put teeth in their heads," says Howard Sharpe. "I'd give 'em my own money, tell 'em, go buy shirts and socks. Some of 'em could buy and sell me now."

The ones who go to college come back at Christmas to show off boyfriends or girlfriends, and then, later, some settle down in town and lend their voices to the chorus in the bleachers. Coaches come home to cold meals and roll stiffly into bed, having offered up their own aging bodies for teenagers to slam up against in practice. When observers portray community high school basketball as the last breath of fresh air left in the game, it is here, in the bond between good, caring coaches and their players, that the observation seems most true.

Skip Collins is in the beginning of his annual worst day of the year. He looks it, too, bleary-eyed, pale, unkempt. Twelve hours ago his Valparaiso Vikings lost the opening game of their regional and were eliminated from the tourney. A couple of key calls went against him down the stretch, to his mind fouls that went unwhistled. He has been up most of the night with his distraught players.

At 9:00 A.M., having already finished his morning radio

show, he appears for coffee at the local Big Boy. The shades are drawn and Collins is wearing sunglasses, but still the sun seems to hurt his eyes. A teacher of English literature, Skip Collins is melancholy this morning. He speaks softly.

"I've just finished my twentieth year as a head high school basketball coach, and that's all I've ever done," he says. "Every one of those twenty years, I lost my last game. I've spent a morning like this every year for the last twenty years, feeling sorry for myself, knowing that I was cheated badly the night before and so on. I feel miserable. I feel like anyone who has spent twelve months working for something and I had a chance at it and the chance didn't work out. It's an empty feeling.

"It's very hard to accept. Every year I sit down and decide whether I want to start over again. This wouldn't be a good time to make a decision, not after the last game. I always plan to quit after the last game. I think, 'Hey, this is crazy,' they need someone younger to do this, I want to go into the shoe business, I can't stand this anymore. So far every year I've been crazy enough to try it again. You may know intellectually that to put so much of your life and happiness into a game is a little nutty, and yet you do it anyway."

His coffee arrives, but he doesn't seem to notice. "I'm 41 years old, and I always thought I would coach till I was 60, but that's not true any longer. Most people don't realize the time that goes into it. Running on the track at 6:30 A.M., starting in September, nights full of films and scouting. I spend most of my summers in camp work, trying to make enough money to afford to be a teacher. I make about $4,000 to coach. Financially, it's not a very good deal. I guess I'd do it for nothing."

He is asked about the future, maybe as a college coach.

He offers a familiar perspective. "The small Indiana schools would probably be a step down. I have better facilities here. I suppose there are some semi-major schools who would consider someone with no college experience for a head coaching job, but most college coaches wouldn't want a 41-year-old assistant. They want someone who is 25 and looks good in a paisley shirt and with a good tan. I'm kind of between a rock and a hard place."

Asked what he'll do if he decides not to return for a twenty-first year, Skip Collins stirs his stone-cold coffee absently. "If I had enough financial backing, I think I'd like to write. I'd put down a combination of observations and fictional things that roll around in my head. I have a lot of crazy ideas. I would enjoy that."

One official's call sticks in his head. Late in the game the ball was slapped away from a Viking right in front of Collins, who is certain his player was whacked on the forearm. "I never berate the officials," he says, perhaps re-evaluating this policy. "I never swear at them or anything, but I was just in anguish that they weren't better than they were last night. It's like, you might spend your whole life learning to play the piano and go to a concert and begin to play and find that one of the three judges has a great ear but the other two have gone tone deaf but they are going to judge you anyway."

Collins gets up to go. Unfortunately, he has rounds today. As he passes out of the restaurant, two geriatric women, waiting on a bench to be seated, follow him with their eyes out into the parking lot. "Isn't that Skip Collins?" one of them asks. "He looks sad." "Yes, who could blame him?" replies the other. "I thought Valpo could beat Michigan City for sure." They fall silent for a moment, then the first brightens. "Well," she says, "I guess we're not going to the game tonight . . . want to go into Chicago?"

On a Wednesday night in November, about a thousand fans are in the Warren Central High School gym for the early season clash between the Warren Central Lady Warriors and the Rushville Lady Lions. Nearly half the fans have come from Rushville, thirty-five miles away, many traveling in a caravan of schoolbuses. Elderly ladies are decked out in Rushville red, and men who clearly will discuss this game together somewhere tomorrow over coffee have come to enjoy the familiar pleasure of referee baiting. Guys in varsity sweaters shoulder each other in the top rows of both sides; girls band together in the rows behind the benches, a surprising number of them keeping statistics.

This is the first game of the season for both teams. Warren Central is ranked seventeenth statewide, mainly because of their 6'5" center Linda Godby, whose name appeared on many preseason all-American teams and who is an early favorite for "Miss Basketball." Rushville, a perennial contender for the state championship, is this year unranked and rebuilding.

This game will pose an unprecedented challenge to coaches Cinda Brown of Rushville and Sue Parrish of Warren Central. Both are vocal and active veteran coaches, and the National Federation of Sports has just passed the "bench decorum" rule, which requires all coaches to remain on the bench while the game is in session "except for spontaneous outbursts of enthusiasm."

The rule is bitterly opposed as an unnecessary restraint

and an impediment to communication with players by almost all coaches in Indiana. The Indiana coaches' association has discussed symbolic protests ranging from having everyone coach in wheelchairs—to symbolize their crippling—to having everyone stand up and get a technical on one wildcat Friday night. "I'm afraid there's gonna be violence," Howard Sharpe has said.

After the national anthem, Rushville's scrambling young guards harass Warren Central's ball handlers into an early series of mistakes. Parrish, who has a strident, intimidating style as a coach, is beside herself, red-faced, screaming to catch the attention of her players, who, in the heat of battle, have already forgotten to look toward the bench with each change of possession, as was the plan. Every part of Parrish but her very bottom is out of her chair.

As Rushville takes a slim lead into the locker room, the lobby fills with popcorn eaters, mainly kids in jeans and down vests and ball jackets. No spike haircuts here. Five girls from Rushville, pals, are among the contingent that follows the Lady Lions on the road. Rushville's girls' team actually outdraws the boys'. The main reason is that they rarely lose. Cinda Brown's teams have won seven out of every eight games played during her nine years at Rushville.

Between handfuls of popcorn, the girls are eager to talk hoops. Asked if they have any particular heroes, several answer at once. "Steve Alford," they say. What do they like about him? "His legs," comes the chorus.

As play resumes, it is clear that Parrish has made adjustments. Linda Godby's cuts toward the ball are more direct and the Warren Central guards more creative in getting the ball to her. Warren Central overtakes Rushville and begins to pull away. Midway through the third quarter, Cinda Brown leaps from her chair to scream for the attention of one of her players. It is a reflex formed of many years' coaching. The referee's hands form a T, for a technical foul, as Brown, chagrined, finds her seat. Her lips form the word "damn."

Both coaches, as it happens, are seated in chairs with casters, like office chairs, which allow them to roll. As Rushville's plight deepens, Cinda Brown begins, quite unconsciously, she says later, to roll closer to her players. When she crosses onto the floor for the first time, the girl seated next to her grabs the back of the chair and drags her back. Brown, intent, appears not to notice. This happens all the rest of the game, players hauling their coach back from another technical. Rushville succeeds at this, but Warren Central rolls to an easy win. As they walk slowly to their locker room, the Rushville girls are blinking back tears.

The girls' basketball program has made great strides forward in the eleven years since the admission of girls' teams to the IHSAA. Girls now have equal access to good equipment and, in most cases, to practice gyms. Girls' coaches earn as much as boys' coaches. The stigma against girl athletes seems almost to have disappeared. While Sue Parrish chafed under the slurs and taunts of the day, her young star Linda Godby says, as if the thought is new to her, "The boys don't put us down at all. They support us."

Likewise, while an athletic scholarship was a fantasy for Sue Parrish, a tall and gifted athlete, Linda Godby has been contacted by nearly a hundred colleges. Some observers say it won't be long before a school like Rushville features the girls instead of the boys on Friday nights.

But as the girls' program advances, Cinda Brown and Sue Parrish, women coaching girls' basketball teams, are increasingly rare. Eleven years ago, when the girls' program started, only about 5 percent of all coaches of girls' teams were men. Today that figure is about 73 percent, and—more troublesome to women coaches—the percentage of male coaches has risen in each of the eleven years. Most women in the field originally conceded the need for men to coach technique until women learned to coach—as Sue Parrish puts it, "How were you going to teach girls how to shoot a reverse layup if you'd never shot one yourself?"—but had assumed that the first generation of men would yield to the educated women.

It hasn't worked out that way. Indeed, men, eager to get started in coaching and better qualified at that time than women, filled the scores of new coaching jobs. "It was the only position available, and I was trying to get into the coaching profession," says Bill Keller, a former star player and now a men's coach at a small Indiana college. "Why wouldn't I take it? It was a lot of fun. It gave me a real appreciation for girls' basketball."

But a decade later the jobs are still held by men, and women are getting out. "Coaching is too big a deal in Indiana for men to give up," says Parrish. "Nobody's quitting. So all you have is retirees. Now we see some women coming back [from college programs], but are you going to fire men to give these women a job?"

There may be other reasons. "The boys' program has become so intense that I know a lot of coaches who have become physically ill," says Judi Warren, the first girl heroine as a player and now a high school coach. "It drains 'em, they have to put so much into it. I've heard a lot of men say coaching girls is more enjoyable, that girls are more receptive and eager to learn. They give you feedback, they praise you. If the guys are in this to help our program, I have no complaint. But if they're just taking over a job because it's something to do, and they see it as a step down, that upsets me."

"Most of the women who are in it are single," says Cinda Brown, whose two stepchildren are grown. "It's so demanding, I don't see how anyone could be a coach and raise kids." "Who's going to take care of the kids?" asks Parrish, who describes herself as "unmarried and the mother of twelve." "How many husbands are going to stay home on Saturday for three and a half hours taking care of kids while Mom's coaching?" Parrish's voice is rising to a bench level. "How many men will put the meals on the table, pick the kids up from the baby-sitter and get all that ready by the time Mom comes home after practice?"

Well, at least one. Jim Rosenberg does well with macaroni and cheese and fried chicken, but his *pièce de résistance* is scalloped potatoes. "It's not out of the box, either," boasts his wife, Sharon, coach of the Carmel High School Lady Greyhounds.

Sharon and Jim Rosenberg are the parents of one son, Brian, 4. Now in her tenth year as a head coach, Sharon thought about getting out the year Brian was born. But like so many Hoosiers, she loved coaching basketball, and she is good at it, having won about 60 percent of her games at Carmel. After a long search, the Rosenbergs found a day-care provider who could keep Brian till 6:00, and Sharon went back to the bench.

Jim is a restaurateur who is able to arrange somewhat flexible work hours. In a typical week during the season, there are at least two evening games, one night of scouting and several practices. Sharon takes Brian with her on scouting trips. "He loves it," she says. "He's good for about a half, but that's long enough for me to learn the other teams' patterns."

Meals are the biggest headache. The Rosenbergs try to have a family dinner at least two nights a week. Sharon prepares two or three meals for the week on Sundays and then leaves notes for Jim, who often has dinner waiting on the table when she comes home from practice. "We don't even own a microwave," she says proudly.

"The key is your husband," says Sharon Rosenburg. "Their hours, their patience. Except for having to hear all my frustrations, Jim's happy I'm doin' it. He helps out any way he can. If I practice till 7:00, he'll wait until 8:00 to go in. In the heat of the season it gets hectic. All your holidays are taken up with practices. It's tough trying to be super-mom, making sure Brian gets to the zoo. We love him and we feel guilty that we're denying him things."

"There are a bunch of women getting out of coaching," she says. "A man can pack up the family. A woman can't say, 'Oh, honey, I've got a job in Evansville.' Women are being replaced by men. For one thing, I think fathers feel girls respond better to a man. They think men give more discipline. It's always the dads who are in here yellin' after the little girl goes home cryin'. The dads are always in your face, especially the ones who played ball."

Men and women agree that coaching high school girls is completely different from coaching high school boys. "Girls are *so* emotional," says Judi Warren. "If they've had a spat with their boyfriend just before the game, they're gone for the game. The hardest thing to do in girls' basketball is to keep 'em steady.

"A lot of times a coach really needs to be close to the players. The community won't always accept a guy coach givin' a girl a big hug or smackin' 'em on the butt. I'm not sure a girl would be as open with a guy in talking about personal things as my players would with me. Part of coaching is getting kids ready for society, getting them ready mentally and emotionally."

"Three of my starters were sobbing tonight," says Cinda Brown, "not crying, sobbing tears. They don't handle criticism nearly as well, but they work harder. Big macho guys, nobody can tell them what to do, but girls are ready to do anything you tell them to. I can't remember ever having to tell a player not to shoot so much, I have to tell them *to* shoot. They emphasize teamwork. They don't care who scores the points, they want to win."

"If you had two guys that didn't like each other," says Parrish, "they're gonna go in the locker room and cuss each other out and more than likely belt each other. Then they'll go out on the floor and pass the ball to each other. But it's just not normal for 14- to 18-year-old girls to confront the people who are causing them problems."

And there's makeup. "They want to know in the morning if we're gonna sweat and how much," says Sharon Rosenberg. "They need to gauge their time for makeup. They're basic Max Factor girls; a base and some blush, mascara and eye shadow. It's water-base; you'll look down during a workout and see white stuff on their sweats."

Judi Warren agrees that matters such as makeup can be a pain, but not as big a pain as the stresses that go with an all-consuming pressure to win. "I'm afraid it's going to change," she says. "I'm afraid that girls' basketball is going to become like the guys'. In a way, I hate to see it. It's getting hard-nosed and very disciplined. In a way, I like that, and in a way, there are some things I'd like to keep for ourselves, the emotions, the femininity."

Seventy boys and girls, second- and third-graders, watch the old man. Eyes bright, faces upturned, they listen intently. "Now, pay attention," he says. "Here's the way we

Sharon Rosenberg and son Brian on a scouting trip. *(Wayne Mahana)*

Be all that you can be: Indiana University Coach Bobby Knight dresses down DelRay Brooks, who later transferred to Providence College. *(John Terhune)* (RIGHT)

Living legend Howard Sharpe savors one of the more than seven hundred games he has won as a high school coach in Indiana. *(Courtesy Bob Williams)* (INSET AT RIGHT)

do it. Come out on the floor right now and get in a circle around one of the players." Howard Sharpe has all twelve of his North Knox High varsity players out at nine on a Saturday morning to work with the kids. "Now pay attention to Mark Dillon here, Mark's gonna loosen you up." Dillon, a 6'3" junior center, leads the children through some stretching exercises.

"Now. First group, come up to the center. Okay, I want you to dribble the ball around the cone in the center. Okay? Now, you don't slap the ball, you *push* it. Push. Push. Push. Push." A yellow-haired girl in a red leotard steers the ball around, sometimes with two hands, while Sharpe and his players shout encouragement. Then the kids try to push two balls at once, and then while crawling on their knees, changing hands if they can. "Push. Push. Push. Push," Sharpe says, following them around the cone. When they finish he pats them on the head. "Oh, you're doin' better *all* the time," he says to one beaming child "Look how you've got better since last Saturday, even."

An hour later, fourth- and fifth-graders take the court, followed an hour later by fifth- and sixth-graders. At noon, Howard Sharpe starts off for home.

Each day Sharpe, 70, commutes 104 miles to North Knox High from his home outside Terre Haute. He drives alone, often in winter darkness along a hilly two-lane road, morning and night, and back in to work with the little kids on weekends. It is a regimen that would break many younger men, but no one alive could know what it means. For Howard Sharpe is really driving a road of his own. There is only one car ahead, and it is getting bigger every day in his headlights.

Sharpe is closing in on a legend. On a Sunday morning in November 1985, he had won 717 games as an Indiana high school coach, or, as he puts it, "My kids have won 717 and I've lost 327." That's seventeen games shy of the all-time Hoosier high school win record, set between 1931 and 1967 by the late Marion Crawley, mainly at Lafayette Jefferson High School.

Except as master coaches, Crawley and Sharpe couldn't have been less alike. Crawley, who died in 1982, was a model of self-control. "Just by his presence on the bench, Crawley was one of the game's biggest intimidators," referee Don McBride has said. "He didn't have to do or say anything to get your attention."

The vintage Sharpe was a shrewd, driven, combative man, a man who paced the sidelines baiting referees, probing for any angle, arousing and orchestrating the passions of everyone in the gym. "You think Bobby Knight is wild," Sharpe chuckles, "he's a pussycat compared to me before I finally grew up."

Sharpe is a short, compact man, given to suspenders in his few leisure hours. He has a precise, absorptive mind and a phenomenal memory for statistical detail. One of his many inventions is still bringing in royalties. When, at the county fair, you toss a basketball at a rim that seems too small and which offers no backboard against which to gauge distance, you are probably surrendering quarters to the "Sharpie."

He grew up in a rough town in rough times. "I bought my first set of sneakers at Seventh and Broadway in Gary, sixty-two years ago," he says. "I started high school in 1929. There was nothin' to do in the Depression but play. I didn't get this flat nose from watchin' TV." His heroes were his coaches, strong men who in turn made him want to coach. He worked his way through Indiana State Teachers College and coached at three small rural schools before settling for forty years at Terre Haute Gerstmeyer—later renamed Terre Haute North—and now North Knox.

In part, Sharpe's daily journey is a quest for personal redemption. While Crawley won four state titles, Sharpe's marvelous Gerstmeyer teams, four of which made it to the state finals, never won. In fact, Sharpe is best known in Hoosierland for a game his team lost. It is not enough to say that it was a one-point, last-shot loss in the only chance he ever had, or probably ever will have, for the brass ring. You have to know what happened.

In 1953, three members of Sharpe's Gerstmeyer starting five were members of the same family. There were the identical twins, Harley and Arley Andrews, and their younger uncle, Harold. Sharpe made it even more confusing. He gave Arley number 34 and Harley number 43. Angler that he was, Sharpe was forever accused of changing their jerseys at halftime to protect whichever twin was in foul trouble.

Until the final game, Gerstmeyer had had only one real scare on the tournament trail. They fell behind against Evansville Central by sixteen at the half in the semistate. Fans in Indianapolis received the premature announcement of a great upset, something along the lines of Dewey licking Truman.

After delivering a crash course on defensive positioning, Sharpe, wrought up, marched out of the dressing room to begin the second half. Harley caught his elbow. "Coach," he said, "you're gettin' too excited. We're only eight shots behind." Then he went out and made 5 long shots in a row, turning the tide.

Early in the game for the state championship, against South Bend Central at Butler Fieldhouse, a foul was whistled against Harley. The official flashed the hand signal four-three, four-three, but the scorer mistakenly assigned it to Arley, number 34. Sharpe noticed the error and protested furiously, but they would not change it. Saddled with an extra foul, Arley—the team's best shooter—sat out much of the third quarter and fouled out with only twenty-eight seconds gone in the fourth quarter.

Still, they had a chance. South Bend Central led 42–41 with seventeen seconds left. Gerstmeyer forced a turnover. "In those years," recalls Sharpe, the words coming slowly, because this is a memory with some genuine pain left, "the clock still ran on a violation. So we ran over to get the ball and they rolled the damn ball clear across the court. We threw it in and got a shot at it with four seconds left to go."

Indianapolis sportswriter Bob Williams described those four seconds. "If one watches the film [of that game] carefully, a small man is standing in front of the Gerstmeyer bench. He watches the ball, leans with it, almost begging it to score. The shot hits the back of the flange and pops away. The man immediately throws his hands to his head. It is basketball agony at its most painful."

"Well, my God, that's what I lived for," says Sharpe, his eyes wide. "I've tried all these years to win it, that's been the goal. My God, it almost killed me. It's been the most disappointing thing in my life." He is silent for a while, and then he brightens. "I guess it wasn't meant to be," he says. "Actually, people have treated me nicer for it than if I would have won."

In 1982 the Vigo County school board forced Sharpe, then 66, to resign his coaching position of forty years. Former players poured into Terre Haute to battle for their coach, but they couldn't save him. Thirty wins behind Crawley, it looked like the end had come. Months later he was fighting for his life in double-bypass heart surgery.

But someone seemed to be looking after Sharpe. He survived that operation and, later, another. One day the phone rang. It was the athletic director of North Knox High School, fifty-two miles away, wondering if he'd consider coaching their basketball team as a lay coach, without pay, and teaching the region's children how to play. He had his teacher's pension and Social Security, money didn't matter. "They gave me the title 'Athletic Coordinator/Basketball Coach," laughs Sharpe. This, in Indiana, is like "Altar Boy/Pope."

So Sharpe set out after Crawley again. North Knox is a typical Indiana school with an enrollment of 558 students, a gym that holds 4,400 and some very rabid fans. Sharpe's young team won only three games the first year. There was grumbling. They thought the old man was supposed to know something. Then, last year, he went 10–10, lost the sectional in an overtime and calmed most of his detractors. Now he's junior-loaded and optimistic.

"I got nice kids," he says, "good kids." He begins to tick them off on his thick fingers. "The one big one is a year behind in development, not a blue chipper, but I'll send him to some college, get him part of his education. Then I got a scrambler, shoots every time he can see it. I tell him sometimes I'm going to wring his arm. Another kid, his biggest trouble is himself. He gets down on himself. He's one of those guys who always wants to fake, drive and take a jump shot. Then I have a real nice kid. They own all the orchards down here. About 6'2", good student, a pretty good team player. Then I have a kid, a real screwball, has a crazy shot. I got a left-handed kid, throws watermelons all summer. He plays better when I let him sit awhile."

He is asked how coaching Indiana kids has changed in a half-century. "Used to be," he says, "you were the leader of your community if your son played on the basketball team. Now, kids'll come up to me and say, I've got better things to do, they'll drop out. Well, that's fine with me. 'Cause when I walk across that line to practice, that floor is *sacred*."

Maybe there is no one left who can understand what Friday night means to Howard Sharpe. "This is not just a game to me," he explains, his voice filled with emotion, "it's a *science*. You see, I've got to have the ball 1,460 times a season, with .885 points per possession, or I'm not even in it." Sensing that he is losing his guest, he leans back. "Ah, it's like bakin' a cake," he says, smiling. "You put so much flour in and so much sugar in. Well, you got to put so much rebounding in . . ."

Had he been born a century and a half later, Abraham Lincoln, who grew up a county or two away in southen Indiana, might well have wanted to play for Howard Sharpe. At 6'4" and 180 pounds, smart and strong, Lincoln almost certainly would have made the North Knox varsity basketball team, probably sending Mark Dillon to the bench.

Like all of Sharpe's players, Lincoln's hair would have been cropped neatly. He would have handed the ball to the referee with a polite "Thank you." He would have learned that there is only one way to shoot a free throw, with your index finger on the valve stem. A pouting expression would have meant the bench. And Sharpe almost certainly could have got the kid a scholarship somewhere, maybe at ISU.

"I'd sure be willing to take seventeen and tie him this year," says Sharpe, his thoughts returning to Crawley. "But I can't because God didn't give me the ability. I'll get a dozen."

He is asked how much the record means to him. In an

age where others pursuing records drone on about playin' 'em one game at a time, Howard Sharpe is a breath of fresh air. "Wouldn't you want it?" he demands. "Wouldn't you want to be mentioned with the best?" He describes how it feels to walk into a high school gym on Friday night, game night, his night: "Practically everyone in that gym last night came up and shook my hand and treated me with respect. I'm supposed to be a legend. They say there's none better. I like that, wouldn't you?"

A drive from French Lick to Indianapolis starts with a stop at Sunoco, where a fill-up gets you a copy of "Bob Knight's Basketball Tips." Just south of Bedford, radio station WFPC reports that Bob Knight, "wearing grey slacks, a white, open-collared shirt and the traditional red sweater," had been the very special guest of the Pike County Chamber of Commerce just the evening before.

The "It's Knight Time," bumper stickers thin out north of Bloomington, around Martinsville, but Knight himself surfaces on WIBC in Indianapolis to state flatly that he'd really rather drive a Buick. Likes the way it handles. Something in his voice says that if you're dumb enough not to at least test-drive it, that's your problem.

Indiana's only resident national celebrity is a basketball coach. Not since Alfred Kinsey opened the Institute for Sex Research on the Bloomington campus, causing parents to send their kids to Purdue and Ball State and ISU instead, has anybody created so much attention at Indiana University as Bobby Knight. Asked by *Playboy* magazine if he ever thought about running for political office, Knight replied, perhaps hinting, that he'd prefer to be appointed Senator.

One reason for his grip on Hoosierland is that his basketball teams win. Indiana has won two national championships in Knight's fourteen seasons as head coach, and an injury kept the Hoosiers from what probably would have been another. Even in the seasons when Indiana University does not have a national powerhouse, Knight's teams, stocked mainly with kids from Midwestern towns, seem to overachieve. His best teams are seamless units of unselfish athletes, inspired players who very obviously value the team above themselves.

Another reason is that his explosive temper keeps Hoosiers on their toes. The cable now delivers the IU games to a statewide audience. Cameras focus obsessively on him, alert for a violent or theatrical reaction to an official's call or a close-up of a player's face as Knight chews him out. With luck, an object might go by, or Knight might grab a fistful of a player's jersey. It's like watching the Indianapolis 500: get up for a beer and you might miss a spin.

Knight has turned Indiana into his stage. His antics have polarized Hoosiers. You're for him or against him, but you can't ignore him. "Now, I'm a Bobby Knight man, don't get me wrong" is a common Hoosier prelude. Hoosiers applaud him for making his players succeed academically and for decrying the moral slime of big-time college sports. They are prayerfully grateful to him for restoring Indiana basketball to national prominence after a period of decline.

Still others wince as they watch Knight loom over a seated kid, flanks shaking like a great bear, ripping into him as the boy looks away. Tension builds around the cable: I'd never let my kid play for him, someone'll say. I wouldn't hold my breath until Knight comes after your kid, comes a reply. One thing's for sure: nobody would like to be the kid on the screen.

Knight has become the State Dad, the old-fashioned, woodshed kind. An IU game has become a referendum on discipline, a debate on corporal punishment. Indiana families gather in the den for the games, often bickering in front of the set when Knight explodes, hawks versus doves, bleeding hearts against hard-liners, positions calcifying as the season wears on.

Knight seems to cultivate a master/warrior relationship with his players, creating a world in which a coach is necessary to make players be all that they can be. Even beyond individual excellence, a team is an elusive, half-mystical connection of undefeatable individuals, an organism that changes shape and density to accommodate any challenge.

Indiana University practice sessions, which are closed to the press and public, are presumed to be a form of boot camp, a place where Special Forces are trained. Not all recruits can take it; more than a few have dropped out.

"Veteran players did a good job of preparing me," says Steve Alford, Knight's current star, "like what to expect and how many practices there would be. But I don't think you actually realize what it's like until you go through it. He brings the most out of you as a player and as an individual. He's not going to tell you a whole lot, you just have to understand what he wants to get done."

Not surprisingly, Knight came to Indiana from West Point. In 1971, after fielding a series of unyielding defensive teams for the Army, Knight decided to move on if the right opportunity came. Indiana hired him in the wake of a near-mutinous turmoil with racial overtones. They needed a disciplinarian.

The beginning was rocky. Trustees, alumni, players and fans had come to identify Indiana University basketball with Branch McCracken's high-scoring pack of thoroughbreds.

McCracken had believed that part of his team's duty was to entertain the fans. Win or lose, IU fans were usually chanting "we want a hundred" at the end of the game. It was a source of statewide pride.

By contrast, Knight gave them probing, patient opportunists, content to pass the ball until they could create a likely shot. Knight dismisses the tension, saying, "I just said, this is the way we're gonna play, and that's the way we played." But for a few weeks Hoosierland was in turmoil.

They lost their first four conference games, and the crowds booed. "I saw the first conference game he ever played at Indiana," recalls former IHSAA Commissioner Phil Eskew. "Some guy stood up behind me and said, "Can't we just have *one* fast break?" At the end of one game, with the score 59–40, fans started chanting, "We want a hundred,"

But Knight turned it around. Indiana won nine of its last ten games and went to the National Invitational Tournament. In 1975 and 1976, Knight built beautiful teams, consisting of strong individuals who shared a common vision of excellence, his vision.

The success of those teams and the power of their coach revolutionized the high school game in Indiana. It's a high-tech, slow-paced, half-court game now in Indiana high schools. Knight and his assistants fan out each summer into a network of camps and clinics, briefing high school coaches on optimal screening angles, offensive rotations, and help-side, man-to-man defense.

High school coaches most often describe Knight as a fraternal man, a man who returns calls, makes his assistant coaches available, helps personally if asked. Like fans and parents, some feel ambivalent about his approach to discipline. "I don't like his aggressiveness toward players," says Carmel girls' coach Sharon Rosenberg. "But he keeps them working and gives them a cause. He creates discipline. There is no woman to compare him to."

"I've heard coaches say, 'Well, I wouldn't let one of *my* players play for Bobby Knight,' " says Bob Collins, sports editor of the Indianapolis *Star*. "But when Bobby Knight knocks . . ."

The 1984–85 year was especially eventful for Knight. He led the Olympic team to an easy victory, but the Ultimate Conflict didn't materialize. The Russians chickened out. He challenged them to a game anytime, anywhere, but the goad got lost in a vast Siberian silence. Then his Indiana team went into a deep tailspin. He tried all sorts of things to pull them out. Once he started all freshman; later he kicked a starter off the team for missing classes.

The crash came during a game against Purdue, when, enraged by a referee's call, Knight hurled a chair onto the court. "I was going up to the free-throw line and a chair went by," said Purdue guard Steve Reid. "I didn't know what to do."

Neither did anyone else. Assembly hall was riotous. The state was apoplectic. Supporters and detractors flooded the newspapers with letters. Lapsed IU fans declared on all-night talk shows their intention to defect to Purdue. Hardliners closed rank behind him. "Like General Patton in World War II, Knight knows how to shape boys into men and naturally this bothers all the people who would like men to be wimps and sissies," wrote a woman in the Indianapolis *Star*. "They would prefer someone more like Alan Alda, who is sensitive, caring, supporting and vulnerable. Sorry, wimps."

Sensing a heroic opportunity, a legislator from Elkhart trumpeted his intention to introduce a resolution in the Indiana House condemning Knight's conduct. A volley of hate mail from as far away as Texas sent him diving for cover.

Hoosiers reacted as strongly to the punishment as to the crime. Knight—the disciplinarian—got away with a one-game suspension and a coy little apology, which he turned into another broadside at the referees. Later he skipped the Big Ten coaches' meeting, offering the explanation that he had been quail-hunting.

"I thought he had matured tremendously until last season," says Collins. "He kept divin' into empty swimming pools. There's no excuse for some of the things he does. He seems determined not to let people see him the way he really is. If the people who dislike him the most could see the Bobby Knight that other people see, I wouldn't say they'd like him, but I think they'd be more tolerant and not so derogatory."

For Hoosiers, the event was an occasion for self-examination: it was embarrassing. As Indianapolis *Star* writer John Shaughnessy put it, "Does it ever seem to you that we take Knight too seriously?"

An interview with Bobby Knight is akin to a tactical encounter. At courtside of Williams Arena in Minneapolis just after his Olympians have practiced, Knight stakes out his turf. Hands are not proferred, nor is eye contact established. He fixes his gaze straight ahead on some spot on the floor. He is a huge man with a whitening mane—it would flatter a senator—nice greenish eyes and rounded posture. His voice is forceful and direct.

At once it is clear that this is not going to be a conversation. He waits for questions, interrupting as soon as he feels he grasps their intent, and often answers with long passages, little speeches, to which conclusions arrive abruptly,

267

leaving holes in the air. By hailing the Olympians in mid-question as they walk by or by shouting at his son, who is practicing at an empty basket, Knight controls the interview's tempo.

He seems to grade the questions. There are no A's—probably A's are unattainable—but the ones that allow him to demonstrate his impressive knowledge of the history of high school basketball in Indiana might draw a B − /C + . He grew up in Ohio, but he still can tell you where Bobby Plump was when he hit the shot, the score when he hit it, how long he held the ball. He can even remember the first time he heard Indiana high school basketball was special. "A friend of mine named Wilbur Burkey who coached at Smithville, Ohio, had seen Crispus Attucks High School play. He told me that Oscar Robertson might have been the best basketball player he had ever seen. That was in 1956."

Questions that involve race are thrown out. It is a common belief in Indiana's dens and rec rooms and bars that Bobby Knight is the one man who can win without a preponderance of black players. A tentative feeler in this area brings the deck guns swiveling around. "What a bullshit question," he says. "Anyone can play basketball, black, white, blue or green. You can think of a better question than that."

It's not easy, though. Asked if the Indiana High School Tournament has an NCAA feel to it, Knight rises, looking around for someone with whom to share this exquisite moment. "Boy," he says, hands raised, this time seeming to stage anger, the way pro wrestlers storm around television studios, "you goddamn writers come up with more euphemisms and more phrases that you try to attach to things, it's un-goddamn-believable." With the adversary clearly in disarray, he makes eye contact for the first time. "I gotta go," he says. "Did you get everything you needed?"

11

ONWARD

In the summer of 1950, Township Trustee Virgil Turner announced that the high schools of the towns of Onward, population 171, and Walton, population 835, would be consolidated beginning in September. All the high school kids of the township would go to school in the Walton building, and all the grade school kids would report to the Onward school.

Citing a study, Turner said this plan would save the township $20,000 and give all the kids a better education. The towns were only three and a half miles apart, so the inconvenience wouldn't be too bad. "It's my duty to make these decisions," he explained.

Trouble was, Onward and Walton were connected by more than just three and a half miles of county road. They were connected by a half-century of tradition and basketball rivalry. Onward had sent boys to two wars during that time, but there was no way they were going to surrender their high school.

On September 5, when school started, the Walton grade schoolers went peaceably to Onward, but the Onward teenagers refused to report to Walton, all except seven apostates. Ruefully, Onward principal William Helms reported that two of the seven defectors were boys that could have helped the basketball team. The Onward school year began with the brightest students as teachers.

Fearing that trustee Turner would try to take their school by force, the Onward citizens set up a defense brigade. They formed a twenty-four-hour sentry, men and women, in front of the school, and set up an air raid siren to alert the community in case of a night strike. In daylight hours, a small plane scouted the road between the towns.

On October 6, Turner rented a truck for a dollar, rounded up fifteen volunteers and loaded up the grade school desks from Walton. His intent was to exchange them for the high school desks still at Onward. Tensely, they began the drive to Onward. They were detected en route, and someone set the siren off. When the school came into sight, fifty men stood in front of it. Heated words were exchanged, then fists flew. Turner and his men retreated, as the Onward residents sang "Onward, Christian Soldiers."

A week later, Turner returned, this time with sixty-seven state troopers, one-fifth of Indiana's force. Onward, too, was better prepared, having formed two rings of trucks around the building, chained the doors and stationed fifty kids inside. Again there was shoving, and again, this time on orders from Governor Henry Schricker to avoid bloodshed, they retreated.

The state switched to a strategy of attrition. Accreditation was dropped. Teachers were not paid. State aid payments ceased. Onward kept a wildcat school alive for nearly two years, financing it mainly through chicken dinners which drew supporters from Peru, Logansport and Kokomo.

What hurt the people of Onward, maybe more than the loss of their school, was the realization that their small town was no longer autonomous. They had accepted money from the State Board of Education, and now they were paying the price. They were fighting for their independence.

Ironically, not long before, the state itself had taken steps to avoid Onward's plight. In 1947 the Indiana legislature had passed a resolution condemning all forms of federal aid. "We propose to tax ourselves and take care of ourselves," declared the lawmakers. But ultimately, that's a lot of chicken dinners, and the Feds knew it. In 1952 President Eisenhower, knowing Hoosiers love a good road, came up with a real soft deal: nine dollars of federal highway money for every Hoosier buck. By the mid-'70s, Indiana had more miles of interstate highway per acre than any other state.

The sympathy for Onward was spontaneous and genuine; no one would have wanted to be in Onward's shoes. Lose your high school, lose your basketball team, and you lose your identity. For a small town, to consolidate was to be erased.

It was only the beginning. In 1959, the Indiana Assembly passed the "Consolidation Act," giving Indiana townships five years to reorganize their schools into arrangements that would provide optimal education for their children.

"I taught my first year in a school with ninety-three kids," says former IHSAA Commissioner Phil Eskew. "Glen Dale, it was called. Now it's a lake. I taught seven subjects; some I didn't have a license for, some I did. I loved it. The principal taught five or six subjects, and we had two girls, one taught English and the other home ec. All the grades were in the same building. Now, there were some good things about that. The kids got in a really close network with people, they learned about people, more than they do today, I'm afraid. But it wasn't a place for kids who were going to college. Some of those tiny little schools, you wouldn't keep a dog in some of those places."

The law also authorized townships to set up their own corporations and school boards, thus removing the schools from the autocratic grasp of the Township Trustee, an office established in pioneer days to administer roads, schools and taxes.

Few measures have caused such turmoil in Indiana. When communities realized that this was actually going to happen, that some schools were going to be lost, that new ones would be built, a decade of tumultuous public hearings, delicate bargaining and sporadic violence began.

Everything was negotiated: the most immediate decisions were which schools would be lost and where new ones would be built. Often, when two schools consolidated, the new one straddled the border between the towns. Other decisions, though—the school's name, the team name, who the coach would be, the new school song, its colors, what creature would be the mascot—were just as volatile.

Huntingburg and Holland almost settled on "Huntland," but then Holland residents declared there was no way their half was going to be *behind* Huntingburg's. Finally they agreed on "South Ridge."

Likewise, after protracted wrangling, the Hendricks County communities of North Salem, Pittsboro and Lizton finally managed to agree that there would be one school, and that it would be named Tri-West, but they could not agree on a name for the sports teams. Lizton had been the Blazers, North Salem the Blue Devils and Pittsboro the Burros. Round and round they went in shrill debate. At the end of one such meeting, a man leaped up and shouted, "I got it! We'll call us the 'Blazing Blue Assess'!"

When one community in a two-community township had considerably more power than the other, it simply annexed the other's school, name and tradition and kept its own.

273

Jasper simply inhaled the Ireland Spuds. It was like being kinged in checkers. You were no more.

To an expatriate son or daughter of Hoosierland, one who went away in the '60s, it is maddening to try to figure out what happened to the schools. Two books have been written—scorecards, really—to aid the bewildered. The tourney seems a tableau of negotiated settlements. The little towns are still there on the maps. Russiaville still exists, but the Russiaville Cossacks do not. They are part of Western High School, along with New London and West Middletown. There are a hundred schools now with "North," "South," "East" or "West" in their names, and six "Tri's."

The consolidations have also opened the door for football. Basketball took root in Indiana in part because so many schools were too small for football. The consolidations have provided a critical mass of students and resources, and football has come on like gangbusters.

The smallest schools now are religious academies, some established to escape busing. There are now fewer than 400 schools in the tourney, half as many as in the peak year, and some of the sectionals contain only three or four schools. With the closing of the little high schools, most of which had built wonderful basketball facilities, Indiana can boast some of the world's largest junior high gyms. The smallest towns stand bereaved now on Friday nights, widows and widowers, when once the heat and clamor of youth lit them up and pushed back the darkness.

Consolidations have made some of the big schools even bigger. There are now in Indiana a dozen or two corporate giants, money-making basketball machines, far bigger and better financed than most college programs.

The heart of corporate Hoosierland is the North Central Conference, a league of eight schools established in 1926. The NCC is Hoosierland's oligarchy: Muncie Central, Anderson, Kokomo, Richmond, Logansport, Lafayette Jefferson, Marion and New Castle—blue chips one and all.

In 1984 the average attendance at a regular season NCC game was about 6,000. According to the NCAA, that's better than the attendance at three-quarters of major college conferences. And, while basketball programs in some Indiana towns are losing steam, the NCC is still building facilities, although one hesitates to call them "gyms."

In 1984, Richmond High School opened the doors to its new $7 million, 8,100-seat high school gym, thereby escaping the New Castle sectional. Of course there was token resistance to the project, but, as athletic director Charlie Hinton said philosophically, "I doubt if any seven-million-dollar building program ever materialized without some opposition."

The NCC schools compete for hardware and gadgetry, drawing on enormous budgets based on basketball revenues. Probably the two biggest and richest programs in the state are those of Anderson and New Castle high schools. It's the Hunts vs. the Gettys when they tip off.

Each is acutely aware of the other's riches: New Castle has seven assistant coaches, Anderson five. New Castle has carpeted locker rooms and a stereo system, Anderson a room full of video equipment. Both have overhead scoreboards. New Castle travels in green and white fourteen-passenger vans. Anderson has even bought shot clocks, just in case the rule ever comes into high schools. "It's like the arms race," says New Castle coach Sam Alford. "Everyone is afraid to let up. I wish it could relax a little bit."

But gym size is the bottom line. When Anderson plays

at New Castle, Anderson's players and fans have to stomach a wall-to-wall banner proclaiming Chrysler Field House "The largest and finest high school field house in the world." Now there is a face job. New Castle's building seats only a few more than the Wigwam—9,325 to 8,998—but dammit, it *is* bigger.

Anderson's fans have come up with a semantic escape. Paraphrased, it goes: "New Castle doesn't really have a field house like they say, they have a gym. You gotta be able to do several things in a field house, but all you can do there is play basketball. The bleachers roll back at the Wigwam, why, we've even had kick boxing. We're the biggest."

Alford and Held share the bizarre problem of preparing senior players for the letdown most will face on college teams. "Last year our seniors played before 175,000 people," says Alford. "We tell them that they are playing before some of the biggest crowds and in the finest facilities of their careers. But for a student to leave here and go to a small college . . . if he lets himself, he can get pretty discouraged."

Alford and Held are aggressive promoters, men who recognize that they are in the entertainment business, competing for Friday nights with home videocassettes, the Pacers, movies and cable. "The days are gone when you could just play the game and expect people to show up," says Norm Held. "We sell our package. We have to make people feel a responsibility to become an Indian fan. They used to joke that if I don't bring in $50,000 a year, I'm gone. I'm not so sure it's a joke."

And the number of sports, mouths to feed at the athletic table, is expanding, especially with the rise of girls' sports, which have yet, in the overwhelming majority of schools, to become self-supporting.

"Our girls' coach is very aware that boys' basketball pays for all the freight," says Held. "I never have any conflict as far as the gym is concerned. I try to be very good to them and make the gym available whenever we can. At the same time, you know, it's kind of like a great pianist: if he's going to play the piano, he'd best be able to practice. If we don't practice, we don't get the tradition and the 8,000 people and the money that goes with them to promote the other programs."

"Give me Fridays and Saturdays," says Sue Parrish, coach of the Warren Central Lady Warriors. "Put as much money in my program as someone else's, and I'll put people in the stands. My girls don't owe anybody anything. It's just that we started a lot later. Give us prime time; I can bring in a lot more people on a weekend night, too."

The tournament seems to have passed through three distinctive phases: a farm boy era, which ended in 1954 when Bobby Plump's shot swished through the net; a city era, in which black-dominated urban teams won most of the tourneys; and now a contraction back to the town as the center of gravity. Since 1972, about two-thirds of the players on title teams have been white, a drastic drop from the late '50s and '60s. In 1984, there was not one black player on any of the final four teams.

Basketball in Indiana's big cities, especially Indianapolis, is in a state of decline. Neighborhoods have been shattered by various construction projects, and court-ordered buses have transported players into suburban lineups. Ben Davis

High School, a suburban school in Indianapolis, is now jokingly called "Washington West," because its basketball lineups contain players who would have gone to Indianapolis Washington High School.

By contrast, the grade school and junior high systems of smaller towns provide continuity for the high school coaches. New Castle has six grade schools feeding into one high school. Sam Alford is able to control the entire system. "We start our players in first grade," he says. "We have leagues for them by third grade. We have to—if we don't they'll go on to swimming or Boy Scouts or something else. I go to all the junior high home games; I know all the players. With the coaches I go over the things we don't want, like zone defenses. When kids come through our feeder system, they have the exact skills coaches want. In places like Indianapolis, they have some students at P.S. 101 and some at P.S. 303. They don't have feeder programs."

It may be, too, that the button-down systems imposed by many Indiana coaches conflict too drastically with the balletic role models the NBA provides for young black athletes. Coaches complain that the playground breeds bad habits. On the other hand, it can't be easy to spin and jam and dish out face jobs all summer and then come indoors to a methodical half-court offense in the winter.

Al Harden, 43, has seen Hoosier Hysteria change in more ways than most. Al was a high school star, the anchor of a backcourt at Indiana University, and a high school and college coach. He is the father of two Indiana All-Stars, with perhaps a third in line, boys who were recruited by major colleges in a way that would have seemed unbelievable to him. The son of a small-town barber, Al Harden is today a basketball shoe executive who spends much of his time escorting unlikely young millionaires to camps and clinics and banquets.

Al started early. At three years old, he became the official mascot of the "Lucky Seven." It was a semiprofessional basketball team, an elite corps of Covington High grads that barnstormed all over Illinois and Indiana. Each home game, Al led the seven out of the dressing room, bouncing a ball half his size as the crowd went berserk. In key situations, they called his number. There was the night when the seven badly needed a bucket against the Harlem Globetrotters. Dutifully, Al sprinted onto the floor, leaped onto his uncle's back, and scored.

Covington, Indiana, population 2,800—at least when Al grew up there in the '50s—is mostly on the east bank of the Wabash River, twelve miles from the Illinois line. Covington was the county seat, but blood rival Attica, ten miles up the river, had a slightly bigger gym, just big enough to claim the sectional tourney. Going to Attica for the tourney was like entering a lion's den.

When Al was 8, in 1951, Covington staged a raid on the sectional. Al's dad's barber shop was command central. As Effray Harden took a little off the neck and brought the ears out, customers spat their opinions about dimensions and materials through the lather. Al took it all in.

One morning, the community broke ground on the new gym. They built it together, on shifts, after work and on weekends, the way you rebuild a church after a tornado. Al's uncles took their turns with the carpenters and glazers and masons. Finally, the welders welded the baskets to the standards and the painters lined the floor. In the end it held 3,200 people and brought the sectional to Covington.

Al grew up with his teammates, the Wallace boys and the two "stringbeans," as they were called, Larry Woodrow and Mike Alexander. They grew up in each others' houses and backyards. Sometimes at night, they sneaked into the gym and shot baskets until dawn. Together they played games in seasons, baseball in the summer, football in the fall and basketball in the winter.

The town watched those boys with interest from seventh grade on. That Bob Wallace was a shooter, they said. They prayed the stringbeans would keep growing. When, as sophomores, they went 13–9 and Bob Wallace once hit for fifty-one points, they sensed that maybe this was the group in a generation that could go somewhere in the tourney. The excitement became so intense that they had to sell reserved seats even in the new gym, and it was standing room only every night.

In Al's junior year they lost only four games and won their sectional and regional. Against Lafayette Jeff in the semistate tourney, Covington pulled ahead with a minute and a half to go and gave the ball to Al. He dribbled it around and through the Jeff players until the buzzer sounded, like Marcus Haynes against the Lucky Seven. "Little" Al Harden, as they called him, was on the map.

Not a bad time to get on the map, for Al had no idea where or how he was going to college. After his senior year, both Indiana and Purdue invited Al to visit their campuses. Al was leaning toward Purdue, because it was closer to Covington and because his special girl, Myrna, was there. Still, he went to Bloomington to see Indiana University on a lovely spring weekend. At the conclusion of their interview, coach Branch McCracken walked Al across the parking lot to his parents' car. McCracken was a huge man, grandfatherly by 1960. Al was 5'9", 155 pounds wringing wet.

On night sentry duty, two Onward farmers warm themselves as they guard against any Walton attempt to storm high school. (Life *magazine*)

Friday night, Main Street, Sunman, Indiana. Everybody's gone to the game. *(Life magazine)*

The Hoosier Village expanded forever one winter night
in 1952, when Indianapolis station WTTV first televised
Big 10 games. It was then that announcer Paul Lennon
(in bow tie) first held up a sack of Chesty potato chips
(behind him) and said the immortal (to Hoosiers) words,
"I've got my ticket; have you got yours?" *(Courtesy WTTV)*
(RIGHT)

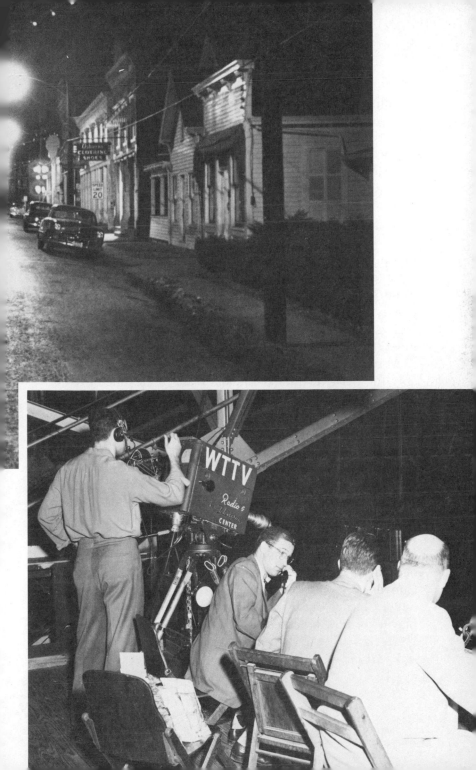

Politely, Al extended his hand to say good-bye. Mc-Cracken draped a huge arm around Al and gave him a little squeeze. "Boy," he said, beaming at Al, "I'd love for you to come to Indiana and play for me." End of recruiting experience. "I just melted, right there," Al says.

This is a fairly typical recruiting story for Al's generation, a time when the courtship of players was aggressive, but informal and personal. Bobby Plump, Indiana's outstanding player of 1954, still has a letter from Butler's Tony Hinkle inviting him to visit the campus. If you'd like to bring all your teammates along, said Hinkle, that'd be fine. Oscar Robertson, known far and wide as the best high school player in the nation in 1956, says he got maybe a dozen feelers. He recalls that officials from one school forgot to meet him at the airport.

At Indiana, as a sophomore, Al Harden played with probably the least restrained Indiana team of all time. Five of his teammates—the Van Arsdale twins, Jimmy Rayl, Jon McGlocklin and Steve Redenbaugh—went on to play professional ball. They started firing when they got off the bus; they rarely stopped running. Had it not been for Al, they would have been all sail and no rudder. "I shot about every other year," he says.

After college, Al coached at a small consolidated high school near Covington and then, with mixed feelings, moved west to coach at the University of Denver. The chance to return home came when the Converse Rubber Company offered Al a job in Chicago. "When I took the job with Converse, it was with one idea: that I was going to work out of Chicago but live in Indiana. Whether they were good players or not, I wanted my sons to grow up with 'Hoosier Hysteria.' "

It turned out they were very good players. Both Rob

and Roger Harden played on the Valparaiso high school teams; together for two years. Both were good ball handlers and superb shooters. Both made the all-star team against Kentucky, and Roger was crowned "Mr. Basketball." They attracted too much attention for their mother's taste. "I prayed every night Roger wouldn't get 'Mr. Basketball,' " says Myrna Harden. "I didn't want everybody prying into his business, writing about him. If I'd had my way, we'd have lived out in the country."

The pursuit of Rob and Roger Harden was nothing like Al's recruiting experience. When they were still juniors, their names began to appear in "scouting services," thumbnail sketches for college recruiters. They read like real estate listings: "Heady southpaw makes beautiful music orchestrating any attack," said one about Rob. "Poetry in motion b'cman whose fundamental soundness is extraordinarily blended with imagination to become a picture perfect guard," raved another about Roger, adding that he is white.

The Harden boys were measured, weighed, graded, classified, observed and marketed ferociously. Al had been a guard, but apparently his sons were something different. There was no such thing as a guard anymore. Rob and Roger were "point guards" (pg) or "second guards" (2g) or "shooting guards" (sg) or, more often, "white point guards." Their skin color was said to be a marketable asset.

Together, Al and his sons charted important career decisions, decisions about how to invest time for highest yield, given the goal of a scholarship at a major college. The boys gave up baseball in order to specialize in basketball.

When Rob and Roger were juniors, they received invitations to take part in all-star summer basketball camps. The invitations came in sealed, embossed envelopes, in-

forming them that they were among America's elite high
school players and offering them the chance, for a fee, to
exhibit their skills to a gathering of major college coaches.

Al was sure he wanted his kids to be able to play big-
time college basketball, and it looked like they were good
enough. To withhold his own kids from the camps would
have been an extraordinary decision, too, since part of his
job with Converse is to arrange speakers for the camps. He
knew the NCAA policed the camps, to keep the coaches
away from the kids. They could look at, but not speak to,
the players, that was the rule. It doesn't always work, as
Al found out.

"When Rob went to a highly touted camp," Al says, "he
was approached by a counselor working there, a high school
coach. He said, 'Rob, an assistant coach from a top university is interested in you, and although he can't speak to
you on the grounds of this camp, he wants to know if you'll
meet him on the grounds of the grocery store downtown
at a certain time.' The counselor even offered to drive him
down there.

"Rob said, 'Sure.' I think this is a normal reaction from
a 16-year-old kid who wants to play major college basketball. So picture the kid, pushing a grocery cart, not knowing
who he's going to run into." The coach materialized, and
he and Rob talked for most of an hour. "The coach told
him he was just the white point guard they were looking
for, that he could come and run their ball club for four
years, that they would set him up in business after school.
Rob did not go to school there. As parents, we would never
tell our children where to go to school, but there are a few
places we'll tell 'em not to go."

* * *

Early on a very hot day in July 1984, there are already over a hundred college coaches in the stands at Rensselaer, Indiana, for the annual B/C Summer Camp, one of the nation's two biggest competition camps. They are there to see a series of games involving about 300 high school players, including some of America's best.

The day begins with the players assembled on the floor for a "motivational speech" by Joe Dean, tennis shoe executive, basketball broadcaster and motivational speaker. Dean's theme is discipline. He begins: "I want you to learn respect for authority. I want you to learn what discipline really means. In my camp, I run you till your left testicle aches." There is laughter. Dean halts it with a piercing whistle, amplified by the echo in the huge gym. "I want you to chant with me together. I'm gonna say, 'Are you fired up?' I want you to say, 'Yessir! Fired up, sir!' " They try it. It works.

Dean is about equal parts fulminator, drill instructor and behaviorist. The hundreds of kids, about half black, squirm but listen. Dean gives them turgid profiles in courage, tales of unyielding men tested by fire. There are Old Testament figures in the desert. There is Bear Bryant. There is even one of Bear Bryant and a few players testing their manhood in the desert. There is a coach who escapes a plane wreck and those who died in the D-Day invasion. "Could you do that?" he thunders. "Or are you too busy smokin' marijuana and sniffin' pot?" Dean tells the kids he loves them, gets on his knees, shouts, whistles, chants, claps and tells them to go obey their coaches.

Then they split into teams. Each camper wears a number. They shuttle through a series of sixteen games on eight courts in four days. Coaches have to be well prepared to know where to locate a given prospect. Since each kid, or his coach, or somebody, has coughed up $230 for a chance to impress these coaches, each kid is at some pains to make the most of this chance. If a given team has a ball hog or two and the others don't get a chance to show their stuff, a scholarship could fly out the window. Coaches fill the stands, clipboards glinting under the overhead lights.

Several years ago, Bill Bolton, a college coach, and Bill Cronauer, a journalist from St. Petersburg, both basketball junkies, hit on a way to make a living doing what they loved. Cronauer devised a scouting service, one of the rating sheets. Bolton tracked down biographical data on the kids. Then they expanded their enterprise into the highly successful B/C (Bolton/Cronauer) invitational camp.

Brokering the nation's top prospects amounts to an extraordinary convenience for college coaches. And since a large percentage of all scouting is now done through these camps, kids are desperate to receive all-star camp invitations.

But then, the college coaches give off a certain scent of desperation these days, too. They are under great pressure to identify and land the best high school players, for the stakes are high. In 1986, CBS paid the NCAA $32 million for telecast rights to college basketball games. Each college in the final four of the tournament got $825,000. So it is that each summer a half-dozen or so "invitational" camps compete to attract the nation's top players and exhibit them, for a fee, to the colleges. Camp sponsors call them "showcases." Their detractors call them "meat markets."

Bill Cronauer is a big, forceful guy, fun to be around, a nonstop talker. He generates excitement. He is the judge, the one who puts the mark against a player's name in the report that goes out to hundreds of college coaches. It is Cronauer who says whether you're one of the top ten, or in the second ten, or whether you round out the top seventy-five or whether you're a "super sleeper," which in real estate might be a "handyman's special," structurally sound but needing work.

Bolton, his far more laid-back partner, is the data base. He sends out the questionnaires to hundreds of high school coaches, asking, among other things, about a given kid's shoe size, religion, best friend, SAT scores, leaping ability and when the whole family is at home.

Their makeshift office, at St. Joseph's College in Rensselaer, is the camp's nerve center. The phone rings nonstop, mainly people who want to know if Larry Bird will be speaking that evening. He won't be.

Bolton and Cronauer are asked to explain how the B/C Camp helps high school players. "They're developing themselves," says Bolton. "They're going against competition that they probably wouldn't get in high school. They're putting themselves a year ahead of time. We've seen kids develop so strong and so quick, how can anyone say it's not good? Now, if you're just going to go out and shoot on Sunday and say it's for the love of the game, fine, but I'll tell you what, it's a *business*. With the pressures on the pro game and the college game, if they wanna play and play right they need to be in a competition camp to develop their skills."

When you send a kid to B/C, you are paying $230 not only to impress coaches, but also Cronauer, who rates kids for coaches. Cronauer is well aware that this arrangement is potentially sticky. "Some coaches say, 'Will it hurt my kid if he doesn't come to camp?' Now, we're not gonna rate him any lower if he doesn't come to camp, but when everybody else is doin' it. . . . There's another camp, without getting into it, that virtually threatens kids, like, 'If you don't come to our camp you're not gonna be on the [scouting] report.' "

Cronauer's credibility as a talent appraiser is a key to the camp's success. He counts diplomacy as an important asset. "When Al Harden had [his son] Roger in here, Roger wasn't havin' a very good camp," says Cronauer. "Al came down and brought one of the speakers down and the first thing Al said was, 'How's Roger playin?' and the coach says, 'He's playin' great,' and then Al came to *me* and I said, 'He can play a lot better.' Now that's hard for me. It's not political for me to say that. He was probably tired or something, but he played a whole lot better before in Georgia than the camp he had here. I think being honest with people in that type of situation establishes your credibility."

Cronauer does not indicate a player's race in his rating sheet. "I may refer to it in a particular case, such as a 'white leaper,' but that's a real distinguishing characteristic; that's not racial. To find a white leaper is something out of the ordinary. Coaches want to know. Trying to provide what college coaches want is our business. Remember, you got a real world out there. I'm not saying a school needs to have a white in the lineup, but I'll tell ya what, it sure doesn't hurt."

Cronauer and Bolton conduct one of their three camps in northern Indiana—the others are in Georgia and Maryland—to be near the Chicago airports and to use some the typically lavish Hoosier facilities in the little town of Rensselaer. "You going to go to some other town in America and find this in a town of 6,000?" asks Cronauer.

But there is a stinger to setting up camp in Hoosierland. The Indiana High School Athletic Association, long a bastion of amateurism, imposes stricter standards on such camps than anywhere else except Missouri. The IHSAA will not allow B/C to run an elite, invitation-only camp. They require that B/C admit any Hoosier kid who wants to play and can scrape up the money. "Indiana is pretty tough," says Bolton. "They are very sticky about the word 'invitation.'"

"What are these people in busisness for?" demands IHSAA Commissioner Gene Cato. "To make money. A coach or a parent wants to do the best they can for their child, it's human nature, but these camps are charging $200. Some of them are ripping it off at both ends: The kid pays to participate, and the college coach pays to come watch the great athletes. We're saying the camp has to be open to any student who wishes to participate."

Al Harden has one more son, Rodney, another white point guard who certainly has talent, although it's still too early to know whether he will make music in a college backcourt. Al finds himself thinking for the third time about the summers of a son.

"I don't know if I'll let Rodney go to a camp like that," says Al. "You play games during one week, and if people wanna grade you and make you or break you they can do it right then. It'd be nice if he's a fine player and can go on to college, but I think we've stressed these scouting services too much. Who knows, if you run a service and you like me, maybe you'll give the kid an edge. I think Rodney can get what he needs at Valparaiso High School. If he goes to camp it'll be because he wants to go learn some things and have some fun."

Friday night is still the Sabbath in any Hoosier community, rural or urban, that can field a winning basketball team. A hot group, pulling together, continues to exert a tidal pull on Hoosiers. And the Indiana tourney continues to be the stage for the little school. With half as many schools in the tourney now as at the peak, the little schools are doing even better.

In 1981, Argos High School, enrollment 247, went to the final four after having won seventy-six games in a row over three years. In 1984, L&M High, enrollment 129, won twenty-five games in a row and was ranked first in Indiana's polls for much of the year. L&M was reportedly assembled in time-honored Hoosier fashion, with the school board firing one coach and replacing him with the father of a star player.

Or take the case of Heritage High School, a consolidated rural school that won the girls' tourney in 1982. There, the good people of Hoagland, Poe and Monroeville found a way to keep celebrating *and* build fiber. Shortly after the tourney, someone heard about a contest sponsored by a cereal company to honor amateur athletes. The athletes whose supporters sent in the most boxtops got their pictures on a cereal box. When word got around, the three towns mobilized to put Jody Beerman, the star of the tourney, on every breakfast table in the country.

In no time, hundreds were meeting together in the gym for breakfast, shoveling down flakes for Jody. Bake-offs and recipe contests put the flakes in unexpected environments. The man who ate the most bowlfuls at "Hoagland Days" won—so to speak—another box.

Back in Minneapolis, the contest promoters soon found themselves buried in boxtops from somewhere in Indiana. They had assumed the winners would be from big cities. "At first we couldn't believe it," said one cereal spokesperson. "But then we looked into it." In no time, the company's investigators returned with the answer: "Turns out basketball's real big out there."